ESSENTIAL CARE of the RIDDEN HORSE

ESSENTIAL CARE of the RIDDEN HORSE

PETER GRAY

MVB MRCVS

David & Charles

**I never dared to be radical
when young
For fear it would make me
conservative when old**
ROBERT FROST

A DAVID & CHARLES BOOK

First published in the UK in 2002

All photographic images by
KIT HOUGHTON
except those listed on page 160

Copyright © Peter Gray 2002

Peter Gray has asserted his right to be identified as author of this work in accordance with the Copyright, Designs and Patents Act, 1988.

A catalogue record for this book is available from the British Library.

ISBN 0 7153 1158 1

Printed in Singapore by KHL
for David & Charles
Brunel House Newton Abbot Devon

CONTENTS

INTRODUCTION

The horse in training is an explosive yet vulnerable athlete, and for those who train either horses or ponies, for any discipline, there is a great deal to know and learn. It is the aim of this book to take the athletic horse from the day it starts work, and to follow it through its whole active working life to retirement. This will not be in a set pattern, but rather through means of common problems, and the way in which they affect body systems, and how to prevent or treat them.

It needs to be understood that every aspect of the horse's daily management – from feeding to housing, from working periods to hours at grass – is capable of having an influence on his well-being. Inevitably the feeding of young, developing animals, when bone is growing, is different from that for the fully mature horse. Yet older animals have their own requirements when they are actively exercised, whether this be minerals that if absent might lead to tying up or simple dehydration that might affect appearance as well as performance in competition.

The idea may prevail that lameness is something that happens only through accident or mishap. Nothing could be further from the truth. It is also widely propagated that lower limb lameness is still predominant, a suggestion that belies the use to which horses are put today, as well as the constant expansion of manipulative and physiotherapy services. The reality is that horses use their whole body in athletic pursuits, and this is reflected in the incidence of upper limb injuries, which, certainly for jumping animals, and even dressage horses, would appear to outnumber those lower down the limb.

Some of this is both predictable and preventable. For example, the horse's back is as subject to pain as the human back, and the removal of pain is bound to make exercises such as jumping easier. Lameness caused by the simple tearing of muscle fibres is of major significance, just as it is in human athletes. Not uncommonly, these two forms of lameness can lead to secondary lamenesses, in joints, ligaments, even tendons. We will consider why. On their own, they cause types of lameness difficult to diagnose for those not familiar with them. We shall also try to overcome this.

Diseases of the respiratory system have a critical affect on performance, and it is important to be able to recognise the ones that are likely to do so. It is also vital to know how your own management can have an effect on this; how you can help an animal get over infection, or reduce the length of time for which it is infected. There should also be an understanding of the conditions that influence air intake. While you might never know what a 'roarer' sounds like until you have heard one, it is well to be on your guard, and to know how to assess an abnormal noise, as well as what steps to take to have one rectified, if needed.

When demands are greatest (*opposite*), there is a need to understand every aspect of the horse's daily management and its impact on fitness. But, even at leisure (*above*), health and soundness are necessary

Training has now, we are told, entered a new age. Whether this is true or not, there certainly is a change in the methods being used, and the type of ground selected to school or to gallop on. In larger, professional establishments, swimming pools and treadmills are popular as a means of increasing the workload – but the dangers inherent in this practice should be appreciated and understood.

Finally, as the incidence of infection increases, almost in parallel with the modern development of equine sports, it is important to increase awareness, to have an idea of the changes likely to mean disease.

The aim is to widen this knowledge to every rider, but also to draw a line where veterinary advice needs to be sought. (We will try to avoid specialist areas, except to mention them when their need arises.) The hope is to improve everyday powers of observation, to turn the attention to simple changes that are the first signs of disease. The purpose is to provide the reader with a means to anticipate and prevent problems likely to arise while horses are being ridden and trained, and to do this in a manner that is easily accessible and simple to understand.

It is important to understand the practical application of horse management and to avoid over-reliance on technology; also to avoid unnecessary expenditure; and finally, to keep your horse going through good management and acquired wisdom.

1 PERFORMANCE AND FITNESS

FACTORS THAT MIGHT ADVERSELY AFFECT PERFORMANCE

- Lameness
- Infection, even mild
- Physical condition
- Dehydration
- Lung damage
- Heart disease
- Lack of fitness
- Aiming too high

Ground conditions will also be influential, and in a competition situation so will the type and difficulty of the course.

It is appropriate to begin with a definition of performance, because as well as the immediate priority of making sure a horse is fit to be ridden each day for purely leisure purposes, this book is about how to express peaks of health and ability when these are needed in competition.

What is Performance?

Performance is a multi-faceted expression of innate ability. It is dependent on the full capacity of organs such as the heart, lungs and liver, as well as other influencing factors such as the condition of the air passages; it relies on chemical substances (mostly carried in the blood) to make all organs work. It also depends on muscle strength, on its type, variety and health, as well as having strong, naturally developed bone; on absence of pain; and it is evident that limiting factors in any vital area will have an adverse effect on the expression of potential.

As is self-evident, the performance potential of different animals will vary, and will depend on such immeasurable entities as overall strength and style. The efficiency of blood circulation is important, and that depends on the working of the heart and lungs. And, of course, such important matters as stride length and frequency matter, and that intangible element, also athleticism, which is difficult to define, if easier to recognise.

There have been many efforts to categorise ability on the basis of heart size, most recently using technological methods such as ultrasound scanning, also blood

In racing the demand is maximal, the horse must be 100% fit to perform to its peak

assessment based on laboratory analysis. These have always failed, and probably always will, because so many factors are important aside from a horse's heart size or any measurable element in the blood. Greater success is had on the basis of human judgement, and in the interests of common sense it would be best if it remained so, too.

In some disciplines, performance does not have to be maximal, and we see horses with movement impediments get away with poor jumping on easy courses. Similarly, horses that have chronic lung disease may compete successfully against lesser athletes with no such problems. This goes to show that horses with mild, limiting infections can perform satisfactorily once the demand is less than for full potential; thus, competing eventers and show jumpers often get away with mild respiratory infections where the whole respiratory reserve is not required. But when the demand is full, as in racing, there is seldom any allowance possible, and here the

In eventing, the demand on fitness is high but not maximal

incidence of bleeding into the lungs is far higher than in less demanding sports. For full and perfect expression of ability, therefore, there has to be perfection in everything: in health, of movement and of fitness. When the ultimate demand is made, any, even minor, inhibitor can prove critical.

In order to learn how to get the best performance from your horse, it is necessary to consider all the different factors involved. Our path will follow the active life of a horse from breaking to retirement, but especially when facing periods of active use, from any form of major competition to, say, a Pony Club camp. The crucial factor is achieving the best possible performance each time a horse goes out, be it for a pleasure outing or an important competition, and the whole thrust of the book is aimed at achieving that.

For the sake of convenience, it is best to start out with a consideration of fitness and the changes that occur throughout the whole process of a training programme. We can then go back to acquisition, followed by starting a horse or pony in work, and follow that with critical body systems, fulfilling the aim in a roundabout way. The idea, of course, is to deal with only the practical, and to interpret text and theory so they can be understood and applied for everyday use.

The Unfit and the Fit Horse

The difference between a fit and an unfit horse is self-evident, though the changes within the body to produce what we see are complex and need at least a minimum of understanding. We can first ask the questions: what do we mean by fitness, and why is it needed? The simplest interpretation is that the athletic horse is trained to a point of being physically fit to do a given task, be that to go for a two-hour hack, pull weights, jump fences, race on the flat, or complete a three-day event. More precisely it means, of course, subjecting the body to repeated controlled exercise in order to develop the various body systems so that they can cope with perhaps substantial increases of energy production.

The training process must achieve this development in a way that allows the horse to express its natural abilities with minimum effort and maximum return of speed or strength. As we shall see, at the more demanding end of the scale this will involve the adaptation of virtually every

SIGNS OF FITNESS AND HEALTH

It is easy to understand why these must naturally go together, since a fit horse cannot produce its best performance whilst it is unhealthy, and nor can a healthy horse as long as it is unfit. The general signs to look for are these:

Healthy and Fit	Unhealthy
Normal appetite and drinking well	Leaving food, drinking too little
Good coat and bright eye	Dull coat and sunken eye
Alert and active, interested and keen	Anxious and bad tempered
Normal breathing rate at rest	Increased breathing at rest
Normal heart rate at rest	Increased/lowered heart rate at rest
Moving freely through all paces	Loss of action, no impetus
No pain or reluctance when ridden	Uncomfortable, has to be pushed

system of the body; even the nerve reflexes have to fire more quickly, as the horse's response mechanism to avoiding hazards and obstacles must be quickened. But that is only one system, and we must consider more fully each one in turn, as we will do in this and coming chapters.

The Influences of Modern Training

It is important before starting out to consider how training techniques and regimes have become more demanding, and the influences these are having on performance as well as soundness. Such factors, in so much as they are new, have their effects and bring with them problems we must learn to appreciate and overcome. The influence of human athletics is evident and on-going. The 'buzz' word is 'interval training', though a direct correlation with the number and frequency of intervals used by human athletes would break down most horses and probably sour those that didn't to the extent that they would never compete. Besides doing intervals on the track, human athletes also spend hours in the gym doing physical exercises that include weight-training and muscle-conditioning methods that would be simply impossible with horses. They can also prepare themselves with stretching exercises that also bear no comparison to those possible with horses.

The question might well then be asked: can we compare human and equine athletes at all? The answer is: of course we can, but there are a few very important differences to consider. First, as just suggested, comes the mental response to repetitive demanding work, where it becomes evident that the secret of keeping a horse 'sweet' is to never ask more than he is prepared to give. An objecting horse on almost exactly the same regime as others may end up being rejected as untrainable when all that is wrong is its inability to fit into a routine that others find acceptable.

Secondly, our perceptions of progressive physical deterioration are poor, and this needs to be changed. Any human athlete knows the feeling of pain, the influences of sickness, and it is a simple decision to seek help, or just to go to bed in order to get over an infection. Unfortunately we do not easily recognise the same needs in horses, and there is no satisfactory means of monitoring adverse physical changes that bring him to the point of breakdown. Some may point out that there are serum enzyme tests on blood analysis, but the results are far from adequate – and enzymes in serum only mean that tissue has been damaged. The results are not specific, and it is time to start seeing the wider picture, to recognise the pains and discomforts that turn a horse sour, and to identify physical injury when it is new and reparable, rather than much later, when it becomes a crisis that might threaten to end his useful active life, or his whole training programme.

In following a training regime we must be constantly aware of signs that the horse is coping with the demands placed on him. Endless schooling may potentially sour a horse, or even bring him to the point of breakdown

(*opposite left*) The fitness demand for pack horses is in their capacity to bear weight for long treks; (*right*) A hunter's fitness must allow him to jump without increasing the risk of injury

Signs of Physical Deterioration

The problem at its most severe is most common in hard-trained racehorses and eventers, when breakdown is a possibility. It mostly expresses itself in the advanced stages of training when the horse is near to full fitness, though it may come later during competition, especially after a fall. The horse will be on full feed and in full work, he might also be spending time on a walker to increase his workload, and he is possibly being ridden twice daily. He may also have a history of recurring lower limb injuries, such as a joint or tendon that is in need of constant attention.

Horses sold after jumping careers often carry serious injuries

In this situation the horse will have lost his action, but in such a complex way that it is hard to decipher; generally more than one limb will be involved, and the rider will very often comment on how uncomfortable he feels. The horse may be bad tempered and irritable.

Generally there are numerous signs that he is in pain, the main one being that his performance suffers, and more specifically, the quality of his work.

We must see that a growing incidence of lameness is also related to more competitive attitudes in sport, more technical fences (as in eventing), and the often senseless drive towards greater fitness. As we are constantly reminded, horses don't appear to run any faster than they did fifty years ago, yet laboratories get rich on our efforts to make them. The breakdown rate in jumpers particularly, as a consequence of both training and competition pressures, is heading towards crisis point. A visit to any sale of jumping horses is a monument to this. Far too many carry physical injuries that show why they are being sold, not just damaged tendons and joints, but serious disruptive upper body injuries that will curtail future usefulness. Many of the same horses show signs of chronic viral-type infections that take forever to clear up and leave a legacy of chronic lung disease, including 'bleeders'.

Besides these problems, our understanding of infection and its relationship to management is in need of reassessment. Infection, if we fail to come to terms with its simple realities, will spoil any equestrian discipline in the end. The problem today is that we look for answers that are too complex: we want science to come to the rescue when it can't.

We change established ground rules for feeding, exercising and stable management, but we don't want to see the results if they are adverse, and we seek answers in tests, technology and injections.

The Aims of Training

- The purpose of training is to increase the horse's capacity for speed, endurance and strength.
- This is achieved through a programme of progressive exercise which increases the working capacity of the heart and lungs, and strengthens the skeleton and musculature in order to limit injury as well as to maximise the speed and efficiency of movement.
- The programme will also rid the body of excess fat in order to gain an estimable bodyweight which is consistent with maximal performance.

Starting a Training Programme

The time has come, then, to begin the positive examination of the athletic horse, and to do that in a way that recognises fault, and aims to correct it. First, consider the visual changes that occur with training; this can best be appreciated by comparing the unfit horse with the fit, healthy one:

COMPARISON OF FIT AND UNFIT HORSES

A fit horse has lower resting heart and respiratory rates, is more resistant to injury, and is more impeded by infection.

Unfit	Fit
Flaccid muscles with no strength	Strong, effortless movement
Shapeless shoulders and quarters	Lean and clearly shaped muscles
Quickly exhausted with effort	Has reserves of enery
Blows easily with light exercise	Has a limited blow after hard work
May become distressed with work	Only distressed if there is a problem
Sweats profusely	Sweats little in work
Big belly	Tight abdomen
Over-fat or too thin	Nicely conditioned
May be dry skinned	Shining coat

PROBLEMS IN TRAINING

Any shortening of the time needed to complete all essential body changes will mean that muscle is insufficiently prepared to carry over-fat bodies at speeds they have equally not been prepared to cater for, and this will cause injury. A fit muscular system – in fact, any structural tissue undergoing training – is strengthened so as to support and protect the body. In an unfit state, none of these tissues has the strength to protect joints and limbs above minimal exercise thresholds, and this will lead to all sorts of injuries in horses that are progressed with too quickly.

Contributory Factors

- Owner/riders who work full time at other jobs.
- Lack of staff in larger yards resulting in shorter exercise times and a curtailing of the all-important warm-up and cool-down periods.
- Traffic density causing reluctance to do roadwork, essential to help strengthen the skeletal structure.
- Failure by many to see the benefit of extended trotting while ridden, that removes in a stroke an essential element of preparatory exercise, the natural way of stretching as opposed to manual efforts that are inadequate.
- Larger competition yards may have some horses spending more time swimming, for example, when this may be the last thing they need. Horses often don't swim well if this aggravates their pain, and some may even appear to be trying to drown.

Changes to Body Systems With Training

While we shall learn in more detail about the workings of the various body systems in coming chapters, it is appropriate here to outline the wider principles of training-induced changes – the general aims to achieve, rather than detailing the science of how it happens. The chart on the opposite page gives a brief explanation of the changes to the body brought about by training.

The need for all these changes is self-evident if the body is to adapt. Blood will have to get to tissues not used in the sedentary state. The whole texture of muscle will change to a more supple tone noticeable on palpation, and a strength and flexibility that allows a greater range of movement, repeatedly, and as needed. Skeletal muscles become naturally firmer – though the precise nature of that, the difference between natural firmness and injured tissue, is a matter for further consideration in Chapter 10.

Clearly, changes occur in all body tissues. The physical changes in body shape are obvious to the eye and are the guidelines by which it is easiest to assess progress or, conversely, to recognise the signs of overwork or illness. The secret is in observation and understanding.

(*above*) Training and a sensible diet will rid the body of excess fat

(*right*) A fit horse copes with sweating and restores fluid balance efficiently, but as a general rule will need electrolytes

Aerobic and Anaerobic Exercise

Aerobic exercise is that where the natural intake of oxygen to the lungs matches the body demand, and the horse moves forwards with each breath at a pace that can be sustained without undue effort or pain.

Anaerobic exercise comes with maximal effort, when the demand for oxygen in the muscles exceeds the body's capacity to supply it. A

heart	has to increase its working capability and become stronger. This means the muscle of the heart has to strengthen to pump more blood with each contraction as well as per minute of physical exercise.
blood vascular system	must increase the efficiency of blood supply to individual tissues, such as the lungs and muscles. This involves the opening of more capillary beds, as well as quicker movement of blood through the body generally. This will facilitate waste disposal and help quicken the neutralisation of products of energy use – for instance, lactic acid produced in anaerobic exercise, as we shall see.
lungs	must make the exchange of gases more efficient, so paving the way for increased oxygen consumption as increasing exercise demands it. Areas of lung tissue not normally in use at sedentary paces have to be recruited and taught to become quickly available.
muscles	need to prepare for increased oxygen consumption, and to store more nutrients for the energy demands that will be imposed on them. Many of the exercises in human athletics are aimed at increasing muscle bulk and strength, thus creating the means to more power to move the body at greater speeds and with greater ease and efficiency.
digestive system	must cope with considerable increases in feed bulk, from a diet aimed at satisfying rising energy demands as well as providing the materials for tissue maintenance, growth and repair. The metabolism must prepare for quick energy production as exercise progresses. Part of this is the organisation of fat deposits, which means the removal of surplus body fat as well as more efficient fat conversion for immediate energy use. The liver must work at peak efficiency to achieve this, as well as in its usual role of maintaining the stability of other body systems through the part it plays in metabolism generally.
body fluid levels	change to facilitate more efficient gas exchange and tissue perfusion generally (the blood has less fluid in proportion to red cells so it can carry more oxygen). An unfit horse sweats profusely and might suffer physical weakness as a result of sudden excessive exercise; a fit horse, on the other hand, copes with sweating and restores fluid balance efficiently after drinking. (It will, of course, become dehydrated if the electrolytes lost in sweat aren't replaced.)
structural tissues	must compact and strengthen, for instance bone and cartilage, the purpose being to protect the body against increasing physical stresses brought on by greater workloads at higher speeds, not forgetting jumping. Ligaments and tendons must tighten to achieve this, too.

consequence of anaerobic exercise is that lactic acid is produced, and this, as it accumulates, will have the effect of creating pain and instigating fatigue.

From a training viewpoint, the difference between aerobic and anaerobic energy production is the difference between a horse going easily within himself and going flat out. The need is to build up endurance reserves by increasing the capacity for aerobic work, while at the same time extending the anaerobic capability to its natural limit.

Both endurance and speed are developed as training progresses and the body learns to deal with (neutralise) lactic acid, the excessive accumulation of which may depend on a rider going too fast. (The difference from a human athlete is that critical decisions on the horse's behalf are being made by a third party, not itself, and this party might have poor judgement; and a horse that is ridden too fast tires more quickly than one that isn't.)

The secret of winning competitions is in proper pacing, and in using aerobic capacity as far as is possible, tapping anaerobic reserves only when essential and at a stage where they will provide enough energy to get the

(*opposite*) Heart rates are monitored in events to detect those unfit to carry on

(*below*) Winning requires judgment of pace by the rider

horse to the finishing line before lactic accumulation causes it to slow.

We can convert this information by comparing pace and effort: thus the human sprinter is nearly flat out all the way in a sprint, whereas the equine equivalent cruises for three furlongs of a five-furlong race and probably only makes a maximum effort in the final two (Quarterhorse racing is more like a human sprint). Twenty per cent of a 16 furlong race is 3.2 furlongs; and horses that 'go for home' too soon will fail to stay.

The capacity for anaerobic running is, we know, partly hereditary and partly training; the extent to which it can be developed for any horse will depend on training and, very often, is the difference between success and failure. The distance and speed of a training session will vary with the opinions and experiences of the trainer, though the ultimate arbiter is competition, and the kind of test a horse will face.

The purpose of interval training is to increase aerobic capacity. Most horse trainers have their own interpretation of what interval training means, but the number of intervals has to be balanced against the nature of each horse, and its willingness to submit itself to the tedium involved.

Fast work is done selectively over set distances and under circumstances that do not compromise the general aim of building reserve, and horses doing it are usually pulled up before they get into serious oxygen debt; besides, lactic acid inhibits muscle fibre contraction, and has the effect of telling the human athlete it has had enough: there is nothing left to sustain further effort. This message stands equally for a tiring horse, which will feel the same pain and have the same inclination to give up.

The Influence of Pace

The horse that runs from the front is always in danger of going too fast and blowing up before getting to the finish. The pace a rider sets is critical, and good riders have to be excellent at judging it. The secret is to set a pace that is as fast as the horse can go without going into oxygen debt. Less talented horses will not handle this and therefore get left behind. However, if two horses of equal ability stay abreast, then a time comes when they both have to go into oxygen debt. Anaerobic effort can only be sustained for a limited period, and this will vary with the horse and might not amount to more than two or three furlongs in a two-mile race, or the final furlong of a sprint. The essential difference is in the innate capacities of the individual horse; think of human decathletes who sprint well over 100m, and quietly die when having to run over 800m.

Horses with 'high cruising speeds' have a natural advantage over those without, but what they have is a high aerobic capacity as well as, probably, good stride length and efficient movement. Horses that get a 'second wind' may have had a chance to ease off from an anaerobic state and return to an aerobic one, perhaps by being given 'a breather' which has allowed the removal of lactic acid, and thus any sensation of pain. Horses that do too much are driven to the point of exhaustion and inevitably suffer pain. Some are soured by it, and there are those that will never allow themselves to go through the same pain again, thus ending their effort, thereafter, when they feel it coming on.

Both aerobic and anaerobic capacity are diminished by any form of lung disease, and horses go into oxygen debt more quickly, and fail to reach their normal performance expectation when it exists.

Steep gallops increase the workload for horses in training

CASE STUDY

The most common reason horses become sour is because they are subjected to pain; with lameness being the most common cause. It is surprising how even experienced professionals cannot recognise signs that are described by riders by, 'He was moving terribly…'. Not only this but the fact the horse is suffering isn't appreciated either, and any protests are put down to a mulish temperament. He is described as 'useless', or sent home.

A more complex expression of pain arises through putting a willing animal to physical limits it is not sufficiently fit to cope with. A horse that has had a bad fall may well have a reluctance to jump again, though many have their confidence restored by good training. But a horse that is not fully fit, or is subjected to a test beyond its capability, may refuse to ever undergo the same effort again

Athletes speak about the 'pain barrier', believed to be caused by lactic acid in the blood. Marathon runners describe how they hit 'a brick wall' of pain. Horses, it is certain, suffer the same sensations. One such horse I dealt with was a champion performer over fences, a winner at Cheltenham, unbeaten as a novice. However, due to gallop problems, he went to a championship race short of fitness, although his trainer felt he was fit enough to do himself justice. His jockey, one of the best, was advised to pick the best ground as there had been a lot of rain and the course was cutting up on the inside, close to the rails. As it was his preferred option to take the shortest route, he ignored the trainer. The horse then not only had to contend with animals of similar ability, but was asked to force the pace and do it on the worst of the ground. He finished third, beaten by maybe ten lengths, but it was the pain he went through that was marked as he blew hard afterwards. In subsequent races, he was never the same again and always dropped himself out when the demand came for real effort. And all because of inadequate fitness and a jockey with a mind of his own.

Assessing Fitness

Scientific and laboratory methods for fitness assessment are outside the practical reach of everyday horse people, and should remain so. Large racing establishments may use blood analysis as a means of monitoring health, though many successful trainers worldwide do not, and the benefits of doing so are far from established. As we shall consider later, the idea of establishing base standards for red cell counts and assuring the absence of infection, or muscle damage, may be the wrong way to go about performance prediction. The keen and interested horse trainer must learn to observe and recognise visually the signs of fitness and health in order to see quickly departures from that state, and detect signs of any condition that will adversely affect performance.

Critical aspects of this will be highlighted as our analysis proceeds.

2 A HORSE TO BEGIN WITH

THE RIGHT HORSE FOR THE RIGHT JOB

Decide if your purpose is to find a top-class eventer, or just a hack to ride and hunt: the answer could be critical. It is possible to buy from the open market, to borrow, or to take a raw animal straight from the field, perhaps one you have bred yourself; the intended use will decide such important matters as size, substance, maybe even colour and age.

However, an inexperienced buyer cannot expect to go to a racehorse dispersal sale to find a docile hack that will be safe to ride – and never acquire any horse without good advice on such vital matters as suitability, temperament, soundness and future span of normal riding use.

EXCEPTIONS WARNING

Take care where particular faults are seen in successful, apparently sound horses: sellers may know a great deal about the management necessary to keep them sound, such as special shoeing, routine therapy, manipulation and physiotherapy, but a horse might not stay sound in your keeping if you don't have this knowledge. On the other hand, with care and knowledge, success might well continue.

In seeking a suitable horse, there are two basic options: to take on a young, unbroken animal straight from the field; or to go for an already broken horse with proven talent and a temperament that will suit your purposes. There are degrees of training and competence which will not concern us here, because, ultimately, it is the active riding horse we are concerned with, and only the detail of how to select him really matters now. Having first decided the purpose of your purchase, then concentrate on factors likely to affect soundness.

Conformation

Conformation and movement are essentially linked, though not indivisible, and it is important to first look at a horse when he is standing still and square, judging by eye, and following set procedures that in time become a routine and encourage the comparison of anatomical points. The horse is, on the whole, a bilaterally symmetrical animal, and it is important that he possesses balance and co-ordination that is visible to the naked eye, as perfection of movement, and therefore subsequent soundness, may well depend on it. In fact asymmetry is generally an acquired, not an inherent characteristic, and the extent of any noticeable anatomical differences of this type may well be significant.

What to Avoid

Aside from obvious deformities and overt ugliness, bad conformation is usually defined on the basis of common sense. First, if a horse hasn't enough bone, it won't carry weight while jumping without risk of injury. Regarding its limbs, if its front legs, in particular, are bent, they will be especially subject to strains and injuries, and the risk of this is accentuated when carrying the weight of a rider. If the hocks are blemished, overbent or too upright, they are too critical to take chances with, unless it is with the very best advice. Finally, anatomical distortions in the pelvic area

By standing the horse up on level ground it is possible to assess certain criteria that may contribute to its soundness and performance. As shown here the horse is unlikely to be perfect, the labels on this example indicate what you should be looking for

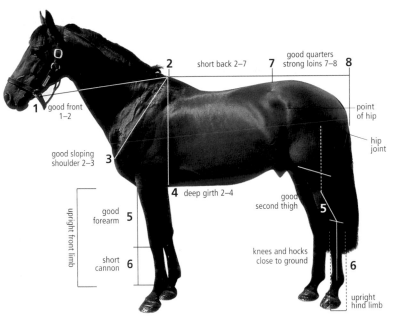

2 short back 2–7   **7** good quarters strong loins 7–8 **8**

1 good front 1–2

good sloping shoulder 2–3 **3**

point of hip

hip joint

4 deep girth 2–4

good second thigh

upright front limb

good forearm **5**

5

knees and hocks close to ground

short cannon **6**

6

upright hind limb

signify the basis of possibly serious future trouble. The ideal you want is a free-moving animal that can express its nature with ease and is not unbalanced, uncomfortable to ride, or a poor performer because of its conformation.

Making a Judgement

First, place the horse on a flat surface, making it stand level. If it is a youngster and is fresh in from the field, bear in mind that it may have had little handling, and may be fractious or just awkward. When assessing it, it is important to be objective, and to accept that a rested leg is not necessarily a lame leg, and that the way the horse is standing may affect levelness at a point such as the hip, where comparisons are vital and false impressions have to be avoided.

Remember, too, that there is a distinction between soundness and beauty, between a perfect picture that will never be asked to move, and a future athlete where the proportions and designs might suggest talent. Such distinctions need very involved judgements. For most experts, this is achieved through acquired talents, not ones they are born with, except in having a natural 'eye' that is nurtured on years of observation. The link between conformation and movement becomes more critical as such judgements are made – particularly as the variety in both physical type and nature of movement is wide: compare a racehorse and a pit pony, a carthorse and a show jumper.

Each anatomical section should merge smoothly with the next, without jar to the eye: so the neck should run smoothly into the shoulder and wither, just as the chest should continue into the abdomen, and the back should provide a strong natural exterior to the spine, and continue uniformly through to the pelvis and tail. The horse should not appear to be in halves, nor should he have evident weaknesses in specific areas, such as a long, weak back. His legs should not be too close, either in front or behind, when they might impede forward movement, or too far apart, where the problem is generally physical strength at the expense of speed and agility.

JUDGING ANY PROBLEMS

Pain need not be a reason to turn a horse down: it may be the result of a fall or of injury, and can often be relatively easily corrected. The critical factor is whether any condition noted in the horse will limit his athleticism, or his future use as a riding animal over an active natural lifespan. Other considerations are whether a condition will respond to treatment; if it is likely to be recurrent; or if it is a permanent defect that cannot be cured. There is little point in buying a horse that requires constant, possibly costly care, for which there is unlikely to be continuing insurance cover.

It should also be appreciated that poor conformation can nearly always be associated with clumsiness and bad movement, and the wise would avoid it.

Stiffness may be something a rider will feel or sense, rather than see when the horse is standing still; but any impression of stiffness in any part of a horse's body is potentially serious, and needs to be investigated more fully when the horse is asked to move – and if in doubt, get advice from an expert in the field.

Assessing the Horse in More Detail

The Head and Neck

Standing to one side, look at the profile of the face, noting distortions that might have been caused through injury, disease or development. All anatomical structures, such as the mouth, nostril, eye and ear, should be normal, and capable of normal movement.

When compared with the opposite side, all surface organs need to be uniform and evenly paired, as do the cheeks and their shape; any swellings or depressions might indicate tooth problems, sinus disease or bone injuries, conditions that are not common – and most horses are at least superficially normal about the head. There is a suggestion that narrowness between the jaws is related to diseases of the larynx, the most common being 'roaring' – though there are no hard and fast rules, and size and breeding may be more important. The bigger the horse, the greater the incidence of roaring: thus in ponies it is uncommon, whereas in Thoroughbreds it is the opposite, perhaps because of lax breeding policies.

■ THE HEAD AND NECK AS A UNIT

Head carriage and neck support are critical in movement, and it is important to note their appearance when a horse is standing still: the impression may be one of grace – or it may indicate pain. Anatomical distortions caused by injury may restrict movement, and will cause an appearance of discomfort in an animal standing at rest. Bony sub-structures as well as nerves and muscles are all involved in movement and balance when a horse is ridden, and particularly when he is jumping, and any interference with his normal ability to function is important, and needs to be recognised.

The neck may be naturally long or short in relation to the rest of the body, or the animal could be inherently ewe-necked or over-bent – neither of which should be confused with postural problems due to injury or pain. What *is* important is to ensure that the horse's head and neck carriage is not abnormal (for him), and that there is a full range of movement that is free, natural and uninhibited from the time of walking out, especially as the horse looks about and takes an interest in its surrounds. Restricted movement, even if it is conformational, could mean a horse is more likely to fall when jumping.

The head and neck unit acts as a counterbalance at the front of the body when a horse is jumping, and the centre of gravity therefore moves with the head and neck relative to the trunk; thus a rigid and painful

BLEMISHES

A **scar on an eyelid** might let in dirt and lead to infection.

A **tear in a lip** might lead to eating difficulties.

Inability to dilate a nostril could impede air intake.

Injury to the ear might indicate an influence on balance as well as hearing.

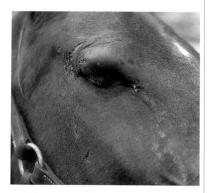

Eyelid injuries can lead to later problems

Warts like these are generally not significant and usually self-cure

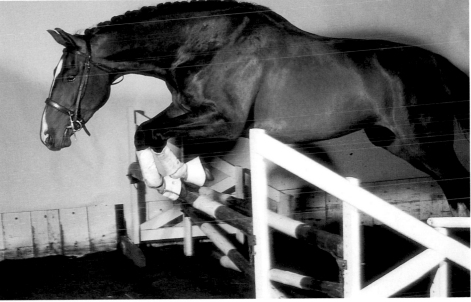

(*above*) The design of the head and neck is critical to deciding the field of vision. The horse in the wild must see predators

(*right*) In jumping, the head and neck are vital to balance the horse

neck can impede free movement and proper balancing, and an over-long neck, besides being inherently weak, is less stable and sometimes even causes a horse to fall. The neck should not look as if it is set on 'upside down', nor should it appear too weak for the rest of the body.

Having said all this, freedom of movement is nevertheless the most critical factor, and as we know from human athletes, all types and shapes can enjoy success as long as they are healthy and sound.

The Limbs

For a horse to be, and remain, sound, there are certain basic principles that are inescapable. Being too big can create difficulties, especially when immature; and having bent legs often predisposes to lameness.

SHAPE OF FEET

Tendon injuries generally occur when tendons are asked to stretch beyond their natural limit, and this would not be helped by excessively low heels (which would reduce the angle of the foot with the ground). Also, when standing square, the shape and balance of the feet is critical in the fore limbs particularly, because they suffer most from the effects of concussion; they must appear level from side to side as well as in front and back profile.

■ THE FORE LIMBS

The front profile of the fore limb should be perpendicular with the ground. A line drawn through the centre of the shoulder joint will bisect the limb down to the sole of the foot, and this should be maintained as the horse moves; the integrity of joints and other structures is dependent on it, and lameness may result where there is any deviation.

From a side view, the angle of the fore foot with the ground should be 45–50 degrees, and the line of this angle should continue without break or deviation up the pastern as far as the fetlock. (This is not the same as in the hind limb, and is explained by the differing working purposes and weight-bearing burdens of the fore and hind limbs, the latter being the driving power in locomotion, while the fore limb bears the full weight burden when landing from a jump, and is estimated to support two thirds of the horse's bodyweight when it is at rest.)

The angle of the pastern with the cannon at the fetlock in the standing animal should be about 140 degrees at the front of the joint; if the angle is more acute – that is, if the pastern is excessively sloping – the ligaments and tendons of the whole leg are subjected to undue strain. If the pastern and fetlock together are too upright, it will cause added stress on other bony structures from concussion.

The fetlock joint must be strong and well angulated, and it should be free of bony or soft swellings. This joint has a complex of ligaments as well as two sesamoid bones attached at the back; it is a common site of injury, and very easily damaged in young horses.

The tendons and ligaments at the back of the cannon should be proportionate to the bones and joints, and should appear as

Crooked legs can lead to lameness due to excess and abnormal pressure on the joints. When the limbs are straight (*left*) the joints have the best chance of coping with the stresses of an active life

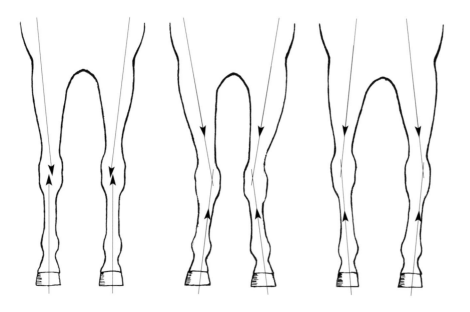

a strong, uniform unit, not 'tied in' under the knee, nor giving the impression of being too long, on too weak, or of being placed too far behind the bone.

From a side view, there should be a straight line through the cannon, knee and forearm when the horse is standing. Backward deviation of the knee is particularly unwelcome because it can lead to crunching of the small bones and lameness, maybe even fracture. Standing over at the knee is ugly, but not such a risk to the horse.

The angle of the elbow – where the bone of the forearm meets the bone of the shoulder – should be about 150 degrees in the standing horse, as measured at the front of the joint.

The angle of the shoulder should be between 120 and 130 degrees at the back of the joint. The slope of the shoulder, as depicted by the spine of the scapula, is generally close to parallel with the foot/pastern axis.

(*above*) This horse has a sloping pastern and appears back of the knee. Ensure the impression is not created by posture, or injury elsewhere

(*left*) The straight limb on the far left displays the correct alignment of the pastern and fetlock. A horse that is over at the knee, as in the central limb, is less likely to suffer injury than one that is back at the knee

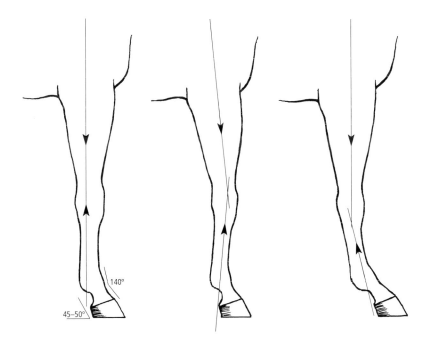

No abnormal soft or hard swellings should exist on any part of the body or limbs. Although some, such as windgalls, may be of little clinical significance, others, such as bog spavin (located in the hock) can be serious. Any swelling that inhibits movement or is associated with discernible changes of action is important, and its significance may have to be assessed by your vet.

The musculature generally should be smooth with no obvious wasting or swelling in any anatomical area. The effects of muscular injury are best seen when a limb is in flight.

Long sloping pasterns weaken fetlock support, just as deviations at the knee can indicate weakness in this area

A FEW GENERAL POINTS CONCERNING LIMBS

Each limb is a handed partner to its fellow, and not completely symmetrical from one side to the other. However, any tendency for the limbs to deviate inwards or outwards, as in the hocks of the horse below, should be judged critically now; and the problems likely to arise are generally more serious for young, immature horses.

A mature horse with unsightly limbs may continue to be strong and sound in the face of heavy work, although the chance does exist that it will not; in such an instance, conformation may affect value, although this would be subject to ability and success in competition. (Without proven ability, such an animal might be best avoided.)

■ THE HIND LIMB

The angle of the foot with the ground should be 50–55 degrees, the pastern being more naturally upright.

The angle of the hock should be about 150 degrees on its front aspect, and the joint, like the fetlock, should give the impression of being strong and well made. One injury that may occur is bone spavin, a hard swelling that may erupt on the lower inside aspect of the joint; it is caused by concussion or strain. An over-upright hock is prone to injury from concussion, and it may also lead to soft tissue problems at attachment points when a horse is jumping. An over-angled hock is weak because it gives less support to the limb in propulsive forward movement.

The angle of the stifle in the normal standing position is about 150 degrees at the back of the joint. This is not always obvious on the surface because of the joint's location in the limb, and in particular the bulk of muscle above and behind it.

The angle of the hip is about 115 degrees to the front when the horse is standing square. It marks the union of the limb with the pelvis. The hip joint is also hidden to an extent by the horse's anatomy in this area, and by the large muscle bulk that is the essence of hind limb propulsion.

From behind, the horse should stand square over its feet, although movement in the hip means it rotates as the limb extends: this explains the rolling of the hips at the walk and trot, an effect not seen at the canter and gallop.

There should be absolute symmetry at the level of the pelvis when the horse is standing square behind. The hocks should stand at an identical height, and a straight line dropped from the centre of the buttocks should bisect the limb equally (as in the fore limbs). From a side view, a line dropped from the hindmost part of the pelvis should, in a horse standing perfectly square, touch the point of the hock and follow the line of the cannon to the ground.

Cow hocks curve toward one another and should be judged critically

(*right*) Each limb is a handed partner of its fellows, and not symmetrical from one side to the other

(*below*) As with the fore limb, there is a direct relationship between conformation and soundness. The illustrations show a variety of hind limb shapes: a normal leg (*top left*); a sickle hock with a weak gaskin which will put stress on the point of curb (*top right*); a horse that is 'camped' behind where the cannon and hock are behind the level of the hip, a conformational fault (*bottom left*); and a leg that is over-straight through the hock, making it weak and with little leverage (*bottom right*)

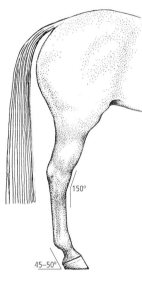

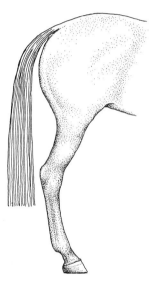

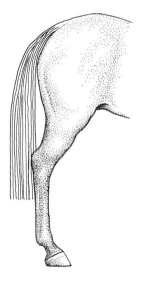

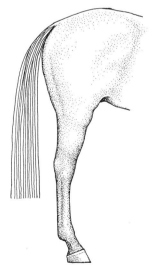

A capped hock is likely to have little significance in the absence of lameness, except for showing purposes

The Back

The upper line of the back should be natural, free-flowing and bi-symmetrical, with no changes in the contours, as would occur after injury. There is a need for muscular strength, though there are variations in type, and few hard and fast rules relating to conformational beauty; thus, for example, roach-backed horses can be effective performers and stay sound, though they tend to be less comfortable to ride.

The whole purpose of the back is to provide support and strength to the spinal column. Also, the limbs are coupled around the axis provided by the spine: thus a long back might be associated with longer stride length, and sprinters tend to be shorter and more strongly built than stayers. The bony spine also gives purchase to muscles from the hind limbs, to the abdominal supports as well as the ribcage, the fore limbs, and the muscles and ligaments supporting the head and neck.

THE TAIL

The tail is an extension of the spine, and often a guide to injuries further up that may inhibit its movement. When asked to back, the tail should rise and be held firm, not go into spasm or vibrate, as it might in a shiverer. Any suggestion that the tail has been broken should warrant further investigation relating to local reflexes and general hind-limb movement (as we shall see in Chapters 8 and 9).

The movement of the tail is an indication of normality in the lower spine

(*top and bottom right*) See the contrast in back length between these two horses. Long backs are generally weaker and more prone to injury

A long back may be inherently weak, and this may be compounded by the fact that the horse's back hasn't just the problem of supporting the trunk and coupling the limbs, it also has to bear the weight of a rider while, perhaps, travelling at speed over jumps and undulations. Its strength and soundness is, therefore, of vital importance. A dropped back is likely to be inherently weak, and may lead to lameness, and it may also pose problems when fitting a saddle. A roach back will cause saddle-fitting problems, too.

(*right*) The back has to support the weight of a rider while coping with extreme physical acts, here the horse is skewing its back to negotiate this obstacle

(*below*) A dropped back is likely to be inherently weak and also to shorten the active lifespan of a horse

The Trunk

This consists of the chest cavity as well as the abdomen, and a well sprung chest is needed to provide space for a big heart and lungs that will provide enough oxygen for a galloping horse. The trunk is not often subject to injury: broken ribs are not common, and although unsightly, are little more than that. Obvious breathing, on the other hand, can be a sign of potentially serious disease (see Chapter 5).

The depth of the chest from the wither to sternum is about the same as that from the sternum to the ground. (A whole variety of measurements are frequently given as a guide to conformation, but it is the subtle differences that count when making a judgement, and there is no substitute for the educated eye.)

The chest cavity should house a big heart and lungs to provide enough oxygen for a galloping horse

(*opposite*) The horse must extend forwards equally with both fore limbs, all the way, from the shoulder

The Abdomen

The abdominal profile changes during training from a pendulous and somewhat bulky state to a trimmer outline; this is brought about by feeding as well as by exercise, though the final tightening of the belly is a consequence of work, and often a sign that a horse is approaching full fitness. Deformities are uncommon, though if any are present, they will usually be self-evident, such as hernias and operation scars – abdominal operations are increasingly common, for colic as well as routine surgery such as testicle removal in rigs. A seller would be obliged to mention any serious operation the horse has had, especially where sections of bowel, or any other organs, have been removed.

Action

After inspecting every side and angle of the horse, it is walked away for about thirty metres, turned and walked back. The secret now is to become familiar with the various phases of movement, starting with the walk and then the trot: it is at these paces that all the essential changes caused by lameness are seen most clearly. In fact there should be no need to progress to anything faster, except to judge quality of movement at the canter and gallop, which may be best seen when the horse is loose in a field.

It is an imperative of normal action that the protraction and extension of any limb is full and unrestricted: each should move forwards to the full extent of its natural capacity, and any shortening brought about by the effects of work or injury should be viewed with circumspection. Also, movement should not be directed to, or away from the natural midline plane, as might be the case when there is pain as the limb moves; this applies equally to front and hind limbs, whilst appreciating that pigeon toes and cow hocks can be found on perfectly useful horses.

Length of stride should be equal for both of the fore, and both of the hind limbs, as an uneven stride length is a feature of lameness, even if the horse is not noticeably nodding (as we shall see in Chapter 11).

Viewing from the Front

- The horse must extend forward equally with both limbs at walk and trot.
- The flight of the limb should be in a straight line because of the way the fore limbs are attached to the body, as though the body were suspended in a sling from the withers.
- The toe should strike the ground before the heel, and this is important: while the appearance to the naked eye, especially at the walk, suggests that the foot falls flat, the tendency for the toe to strike first increases with pace and is easily demonstrated.
- There should be no inward or outward rotation, and the foot must land level from outside to inside – that is, not one side before the other, which could lead to, or result from, lameness.

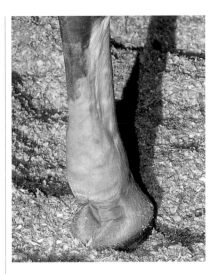

THE EFFECTS OF INJURY

The importance of assessing a horse's natural movement cannot be over-emphasised, as the incidence of injury is high in horses that have been ridden or competed; it is also relatively common in young horses that are in from the field, or recently broken. The reality is, that horses can be injured at any time of their lives, and the significance of injuries such as tendon damage (shown above) needs to be assessed for the likely effect they might have on future usefulness.

These injuries also need to be distinguished from variations in normal movement that might catch the eye – such as dishing or winging – that may, or may not, have some material influence on use or ability. A critical factor in making this assessment will be any lump or swelling that might have developed as a result of faulty conformation. A horse with bad splints, for example, may have a conformation fault causing them; although the problem may respond to corrective treatment.

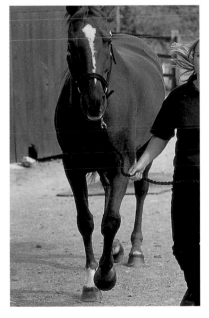

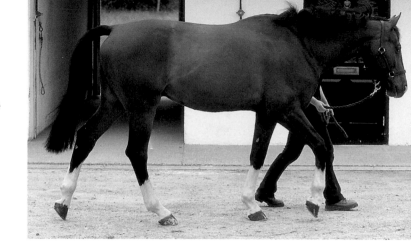

(right) From the side, stride length should be equal in front and behind

(below) Symmetry is judged as the horse is standing square

(bottom) The length of stride is dictated by the impulsion from behind

Viewing from the Side

- The effect of movement on limb conformation is important, and judgements are more easily made about whether a limb is too upright or too bent.

- In the fore limbs, the shape of the shoulder decides, to an extent, the length of stride; thus a horse with an upright shoulder will also probably have an upright pastern, and as a result it is bound to have a short, choppy stride when compared to one with a more sloping shoulder and pastern, whose limb swings through a longer arc from the shoulder joint and therefore covers a greater distance of ground.

- The length of stride is also dictated by the impulsion from behind, which will decide how far the fore limb travels before making ground contact; this will depend on the length and shape of the hind limb. The length of each stride can be best judged from the side: in some kinds of lameness there is often an observable shortening (see Chapter 11).

If the horse is in pain he may be reluctant to step under his body with his hind legs (*above left*), and may throw up his head (*below left*) when asked to trot

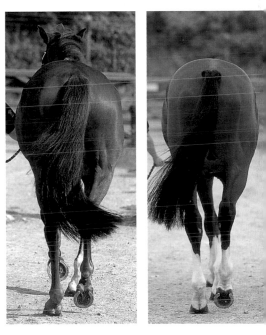

Symmetry behind is critical at rest and in movement, and should be assessed from behind as well as in front and from the side

Viewing from Behind

- The impetus for forward movement has to come from the hind limb and quarters: the nature of movement from behind should therefore be the same as for the fore limbs, with the sole exception that the hind limb, being attached to the body through the hip joint, has a different flight pattern.

- The foot and lower limb is lifted and extended forwards to the full extent of its natural flight at the walk and trot; but because of rotation through the hip, there is a slight outward deviation in the flight of the limb; this happens because the ball-shaped head of the main bone, the femur, rolls through the socket of the pelvic side of the hip joint. Thus the flight of the foot draws a discreet arc rather than a straight line, though the foot itself should land level from toe to heel, as it does in front.

- For soundness, there has to be joint stability as the weight is taken, otherwise the risk of lameness increases; this is threatened where there is poor hind foot balance, due to either poor conformation or inadequate shoeing.

- The upper line should remain level at all paces, unless there is, or is likely to be, lameness.

Taking Advice: Veterinary Examinations

In all cases it is wise to take advice, and before completing a purchase, to have a veterinary examination carried out. This is done as a professional service. The procedure is comprehensive, and intended to find all physical defects. However, while this is possible with most conditions, there are limitations and exceptions (think of developing diseases that have not expressed themselves).

When enlisting the services of a vet, always seek an independent practitioner with experience in this area; furthermore it is unwise to permit a seller to use his own vet in case of bias. Your vet is obliged to inform you of anything material that emerges in the course of the examination.

An already written certificate, even if the horse was examined just a few days previously, is unsatisfactory and should always be treated with caution; the horse should be sound at the moment of purchase. On the other hand, a limited certificate that explains the significance of a given condition – such as, for example, a swelling or deformity – may be helpful, particularly if X-rays are provided; however, such a certificate may be completely worthless should something subsequently go wrong,

BUYING CONSIDERATIONS

When trying to buy a horse, be aware that it is a complex task in which there are many pitfalls. In every country there are individual laws and often varying regulations regarding the rights of buyers and sellers. It is your duty to be aware of these if you wish to take action after buying a faulty horse. Often, being diligent in regard to soundness, temperament, ability and so on, is not enough.

TIPS

■ A seller is obliged to disclose any vices or temperament problems.

■ Aim for a horse compatible with your own experience.

■ The horse's standard of performance must be adequate for your purpose.

■ A horse to jump will need strength and soundness in the back and quarters.

■ A horse for dressage will need good action through all paces.

■ A horse to race must have no condition that will impede its future use.

■ Age dictates the length of future usefulness.

■ Breeding is an important indicator to ability and temperament.

■ A horse that is too small may not carry weight.

■ A horse that is too big may be hard to keep sound.

■ Mares may be phlegmatic when in season.

■ Colts are likely to be aggressive.

■ Colour can be important if, for example, it must match others on a driving team.

indeed it could even be used by an insurer as an excuse for refusing cover on any consequential loss due to the particular defect. Note, too, that a certificate from a seller's vet to say a horse was suitable for any particular purpose might have no standing in today's law.

If any material factor arises which means an animal is unsound for the use for which it is being bought, a buyer would be entitled to reject it, though the reason could not be frivolous; and it is always possible to buy an unsuitable animal at a sale, where you fail to appreciate the conditions under which it was sold.

Further Tests

Where a vet is carrying out an examination for purchase, the brief is dictated by conditions on the day. Within a sale yard, the whole procedure may be restricted by the conditions of that particular sale, and by the facilities available at the time. For example, it will not, as a general rule, be possible to carry out tests such as X-rays, ultrasound scanning and endoscopy. If an animal is found in need of these, the sale may be aborted, or alternatively, an agreement may be made to have a specified test carried out later, and the sale to remain in suspension until that is done. In such a case, the auctioneers would have to be advised.

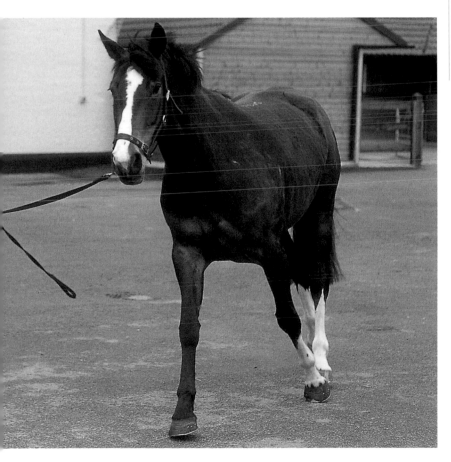

PITFALLS

- Do not buy in haste, but take time to look and think.

- At public sales, horses may not be returnable if unsound, depending on the conditions of sale.

- A buyer is legally obliged to be knowing, which means using advice when in doubt. An obviously damaged tendon must be recognised, as must any growth or blemish that is evident; there is no allowance for not seeing.

- The conditions under which horses can be returned are generally stated in sales' catalogues, and have to be adhered to.

- In a private sale there is more time, but the same obligation to be informed.

- A buyer cannot return a horse because of not liking it after taking it home; there has to be a substantial reason, and one that has weight in law.

- The essential is to be diligent, to prepare well, and to take plenty of advice where there is room for doubt.

(*far left*) A veterinary examination will be a vital step in your decision making process. Although there are limitations, the procedure is comprehensive and will reveal defects the lay person could not spot

(*left*) Lameness is often accentuated on hard surfaces but it is unwise to lunge horses on concrete, especially when wearing shoes. Foot problems will be accentuated but should be detectable without endangering the animal

CASE STUDY

Horses can be influenced by bad memories and this sometimes expresses itself when being examined by a vet.

One such pony, considered to be bomb proof, went straight up the wall when I entered his stable carrying a stethoscope. He had, apparently, had a bad experience and was afraid of vets. The situation was so serious it took some patience to carry out the examination and the purchaser decided against having him, when informed of what had happened.

Another very quiet riding horse was being vetted and seemed the most placcid animal until I tried to touch his poll, which proved impossible. It subsequently materialised that a previous owner had broken a bottle over his head, but this sale did go through.

It all goes to show how important it is to learn a horse's full history when buying, and how useful a veterinary examination often is before completion.

In a private sale, any test may be requested, and the vet will advise and help decide on the need, but there will be added cost involved and the consent of the seller must be had. Blood samples are taken routinely at the completion of a pre-purchase examination now, the purpose being to detect drugs that could hide any evident condition, such as lameness.

The vet will not provide assurances on temperament and vices, and it is in your interests to get these direct from the seller.

A seller is obliged to disclose anything that is material to a horse's well-being or that might preclude normal use, and he or she is liable if failing to do this honestly.

While there are limits to the veterinary opinion expressed, vetting forms a vital part of the protections needed in buying, especially should anything go wrong later. Furthermore the vet's certificate can be used when insuring the horse, thus saving cost. And just bear in mind that although knowledgeable horsemen/women may give excellent advice on buying, almost invariably they, too, will have horses vetted that they are buying for themselves.

A Horse's Value

The value of a horse or pony is affected by many things, even by something as simple as a splint. It is determined by soundness, as well as by breeding and potential. It may also be influenced by success in

STABLE VICES

There are certain vices that will detract from a horse's value:

Boxwalking: the horse constantly walks in circles round its box, usually making a path in its bedding.

Crib-biting: it habitually chews wood and other fixed objects.

Weaving: it habitually sways its head and neck from side to side, sometimes so violently that it shifts from one front foot to the other; it generally does this whilst it is stabled.

Wind-sucking: it swallows air, usually while grasping a fixed object with its front teeth.

cataracts	These are not always visible to the naked eye, but obviously will impair performance.
examination of the heart	Where there is doubt, another opinion can be sought, and further tests can be advised; if there is no doubt, the horse may be rejected on the spot.
examination of the wind	This means that a horse must be galloped, either ridden or lunged; if this cannot be done at the vendor's premises, it is often possible to get a vendor's warranty, which means the horse can be returned within a specified time if it proves to be unsound of wind.
changes in structural anatomy due to back and muscle problems	This is an increasingly contentious area, though the importance of such changes will vary depending on the intended use: thus a horse required for hacking only might not be disadvantaged by an old settled injury, whereas one for jumping might well be.
enlarged joints	These are likely to cause chronic lameness.
scars	Might be significant, depending on their site, and any underlying damage.
skin lesions	Ringworm, sarcoids, tumours and suchlike must be recognised: failure to do so could prevent the horse being returned later.
tendon injuries	Generally indicated by a certain amount of thickening round the site of injury, though may be subtle.
stringhalt	When a horse lifts its hind leg, or legs, unusually high in movement.
shiverer	The horse will show spasm of the hind legs or tail when it is made to back.
wobbler	A horse that is unco-ordinated in its movement.

competition – though it must be said that the most valuable animals in any category not only have ability, they are generally well made, good movers, and sound.

Remember that many horses lose value from the time they are bought, and any significant subsequent injury can magnify this. The buyer must be sure in his own mind that the horse he has bought is worth the price he paid for it, especially if he was hoping not to lose money, or even to make a profit. It is therefore most important to appreciate that older horses are more likely to become unsound, they may not be insurable, and they may have only a limited mileage left for riding. Young horses, on the other hand, are likely to be green while learning, and can be difficult to handle. A lame mare or colt may have value for breeding.

3 ROUTINE CARE & MANAGEMENT

There are certain routine measures that need to be adopted to protect a horse's health throughout his life from foalhood onwards: regular care of the hooves and teeth, and a strict worming programme are essential to maintain him in optimum condition, and when he is in work, to maximise the chances of his achieving his work programme – be this hunting, racing, show jumping, dressage, riding club or Pony Club activities or just hacking about – without preventable setback or lay-off. Once he is in work, further aspects of management should be considered, such as dietary changes, grooming and hygiene, also exercise regimes, and what tack to use.

Care of the Hooves and Shoeing

The hooves of any horse or pony should be trimmed regularly – every eight to ten weeks – from foalhood onwards to maintain an even shape and prevent cracks, as far as is possible. And when a horse comes in from a period of being roughed off, or a youngster is brought up for breaking in, the first priority is to have the feet trimmed and balanced, and preferably shod – and no horse or pony should even be lunged in a sand ring until this is done. Hooves that have been neglected may well be a bad shape, thus unbalancing the whole limb, they will probably be cracked, and the horn chipped or broken to a greater or lesser degree, all of which makes it difficult for the farrier to make a good job of shoeing. Horses are shod, principally, to protect their hooves from excessive wear on hard surfaces, thus preventing lameness that might leave them unable to work – and there are not many horses or ponies capable of staying sound through a working season without shoeing.

Horseshoes protect the structures within the hoof against the concussive influences of speed and ground, but when the farrier fits a set of shoes it is imperative that he preserves the horse's natural hoof and limb balance. To this end he should watch the horse walk and trot,

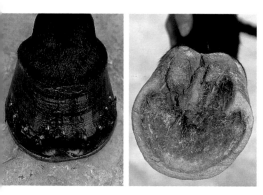

(*left*) The foot should appear balanced when placed in the ground
(*right*) Balance is achieved by correct trimming

Imbalance here is a result of neglect. Once the horn becomes damaged the farrier's job becomes much more difficult. Regular attention is the key to balanced feet both before and after shoeing, because even the smallest imbalance can be serious – for example, splints in mature horses are more commonly due to limb imbalance than to trauma, and so are injured fetlocks.

Balancing the Hoof

There are certain simple principles involved in assessing the balance of a horse's hoof. From the side view, as we have already ascertained, the angle of the hoof with the ground at the toe should be 45–50 degrees, and it is important that the line of this angle continues up the pastern without a break either forwards or backwards. When the line is broken backwards, the toe may be too long, or the heels may be too low, or both problems may exist at once. When the line is broken forwards, the heels may be too high, a problem that may also be associated with contraction of the frog.

Viewed from in front, a line drawn perpendicularly from the ground should bisect the foot and run up through the centre of the pastern and fetlock, and continue right up the middle of the cannon bone. Thus a line drawn through the centre of the hoof parallel to the ground will be at right angles to the upward line. This will not happen if a horse is 'toeing in' or 'out'; it also won't happen if the effective length of the wall is greater on one side than the other.

When the foot is picked up, an imaginary line drawn across the centre should be at right angles to a line bisecting the foot at the toe. The angles may be checked by using a protractor.

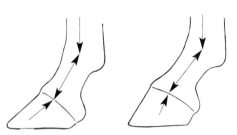

The line of the hoof and pastern should not break either backward or forward

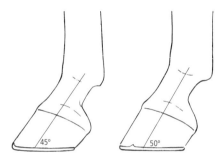

The angle of the foot/pastern axis is more acute in the fore limb (*left*) than the hind (*right*)

(*left*) Poor foot balance can affect higher limb structures. Viewed from in front, a bisecting line should go through the centre of all structures. Poor shoeing can affect this

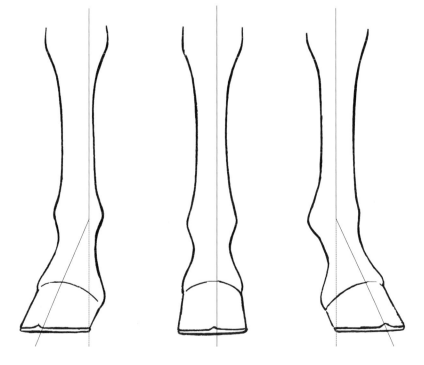

'Toeing In' or 'Out'

Toeing in or out often leads to lameness – though having said that, many horses so affected do in fact remain sound. Splints are probably the most common problem, though fetlock joint sprains can occur, as this is the joint most immediately affected when there is a loss of hoof balance. In some cases correction can be achieved by trimming, generally a gradual process carried out over a period of time; thus toeing in can be corrected by lowering the inside wall of the hoof, and toeing out by lowering the outside (though this may over-simplify the issue). The critical decision will be made by the farrier or vet, depending on the hooves of the individual animal, or by both together, working in conjunction. Correction might also be achieved by altering the shape of the shoe – that is, by lowering one branch as appropriate, to have the same effect.

What is most important is to achieve limb balance, because a balanced foot on an unbalanced limb will achieve little in maintaining overall limb soundness.

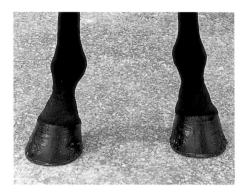

Toeing out (*left*) or in (*right*) places stresses on remote leg areas

The Importance of Grip

A horse's ability to grip is based on the nature and anatomy of its hooves, especially the fore hooves when landing from a jump, or the hind hooves when pushing the weight of the horse off the ground. The capacity to grip is an essential aspect of locomotion, and it is important to understand it. When a horse loses grip with its feet, it tries to control its forward momentum and balance through its musculature, and the result is very likely to be upper body muscular injury, because it is not a natural function of muscles acting alone to do this. Joints or ligaments may also suffer loss of stability and be injured. Very often a horse loses grip because he feels pain, and to a greater or lesser degree is lame; but often certain types of shoeing can remove or reduce this pain.

The whole shape of the hoof is designed to provide purchase when meeting, or pushing off from, the ground, so allowing a contact that limits the tendency to slip, thus avoiding injury. The sole is concave, there are two bars that meet the wall at the heels, and the frog, that is located between the bars, is spongy and wedge-shaped, with the apex of the wedge situated at about the middle of the foot. On meeting the ground, the spongy frog is pressed upwards and outwards, and in doing

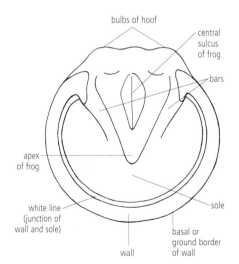

bulbs of hoof

central sulcus of frog

bars

apex of frog

white line (junction of wall and sole)

sole

basal or ground border of wall

wall

The sole of the foot is designed to provide stability in movement this it achieves more than a single effect. Primarily, this creates a wider surface area of contact with the ground, thus increasing the grip by creating a stable hold that will not allow unwanted movement (which nevertheless may be unavoidable on slippery or shifting ground). It also spreads the effect of concussion over the whole foot, rather than leaving any single part to bear the brunt of it. Thirdly, it has an important effect on circulation because it assists the return of venous blood up the limb.

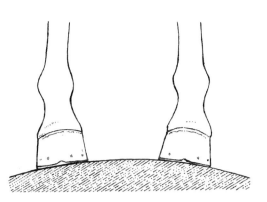

The influences of uneven surfaces can cause sprains and lameness

■ GRIP AND WORKING SURFACES

Good, cushioned grass probably provides the best grip, and poses the least threat to horses from concussion. All-weather surfaces generally limit concussion, but also need to provide adequate grip – and it must be said, do not always do so. Consistency of going is of greatest benefit to a horse, although inevitably this may be affected by extremes of weather, be this rain, ice, snow and so on.

Some surfaces ride 'dead', and users complain of tendon problems; others shift, and muscular problems are more common in these; yet others are on the firm side, but with better grip. Any hard surface, and especially concrete, holds an inherent risk to horses because it causes concussion, as well as providing inadequate grip. Horses lunged on hard surfaces with shoes on risk falling because of lack of grip.

(*above*) Movement on artifical surfaces can lead to injury, making a secure grip essential. Many horses go repeatedly lame on unsuitable surfaces

(*left*) Good cushioned grass can provide the best grip

THE FROG IN THE SHOD HORSE

As we have seen, the frog plays a critical part in helping the foot to have grip when in contact with the ground, and it is safe to say this function is extra important in the shod foot. While the shoe protects the foot, it does so at the expense of at least some grip, irrespective of what efforts are made to minimise the effect.

Shoeing removes the frog, however marginally, from its maximum scope of ground contact. It also reduces the capacity of the walls to expand, and the extent of this limitation is dictated by the expansion potential of the iron, steel, aluminium, rubber or plastic of which the shoe is made.

If the frog is not allowed to expand, it contracts, and any sign that it has done so must act as a warning, as the process is progressive if not countered quickly. Contraction can arise from failing to trim the heels, or from any lameness that reduces frog pressure. This may include upper body lameness, where weight distribution is altered and the horse saves its weight from normal distribution to a painful limb. A horse feeling foot discomfort will also try to transfer weight to another limb, or hold the affected limb in a way that limits pain; this places a greater burden on other parts, including upper limb musculature, as well as being detrimental to the frog. Artificial means of creating frog pressure may cause foot pain and reduce grip.

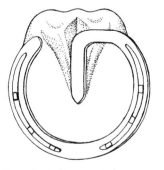

This shoe is constructed to promote frog pressure. It does, by its nature, compromise grip, and is also likely to cause discomfort

The Effects of Shoeing

When we apply a shoe we change the horse's natural capacity to grip, as well as the ground rules of foot/ground contact. This is, of course, an essential, calculated sacrifice to allow for modern horse use. There are two practical reasons for putting shoes on our horses: first, to prevent excessive wear of the hooves on hard surfaces, even if only when coming and going from more ideal working grounds. Secondly, for many of our modern types of horse, breeding has caused a less rugged hoof to evolve that needs the protection of a shoe. If we need proof, think of the way hooves often degenerate in unshod horses at grass – indeed, many unshod riding horses can't cross a gravelled yard without experiencing pain, whereas feral horses cross the roughest terrain without any apparent discomfort.

While shoes reduce grip, particularly on hard surfaces such as concrete or tarmac, good farriery makes every effort to limit the effects of this, both by the design of shoe and the materials used. For example, grip is improved by grooving the surface of the shoe: compare a grooved shoe to a heavy iron shoe with a flat surface, and it is easy to see how the horse is more likely to slip on the latter, which, in certain situations, acts like a skate. Grip is also improved by the presence of nail heads, by putting in studs, or by using an anti-slip substance to finish,

CASE STUDY A young horse was presented with hind limb lameness which turned out to be muscular and was found to be concentrated in the pelvic area. A course of physiotherapy was undertaken and the problem was resolved fully, the owner reporting that he was moving 'beautifully' afterwards. However, within a matter of months, he was reported lame again and it turned out that he had done the splits while being ridden on the road. Another course of physiotherapy was needed and progress was slower than expected. It then materialised that the horse had been put into heartbar shoes and these were causing him to slip when ridden, thus exacerbating the problem. Although the farrier objected, having suggested heart-bar shoes were essential because of the way the feet were growing, once they were replaced by conventional shoes, the problem resolved itself quickly and did not recur.

such as corundum. Plastic shoes can also provide much better grip simply because of the type of plastic used in them.

▪ HOW DIFFERENT SHOES AFFECT THE FOOT

The greater the width of iron in a shoe – that is, the wider the web – the less grip a horse has, especially on slippery surfaces, or concrete. Any kind of shoe extension may increase this effect if it limits expansion and reduces the foot's contact with the ground. The wider the web the higher the chance of bruising also, especially if the walls of the hoof are weak, or the shoes are left on too long.

Conversely, the narrower the shoe, the less there is interference with natural grip; this is why racehorses wear, mostly, narrower, lighter shoes than heavier riding types.

The weight of the shoe is important; consider the saying 'an ounce on the foot is equal to a pound on the back'. Using a weighted shoe is sometimes recommended for remedial purposes, though there is little evidence that weight, *per se*, is of any clinical benefit. The correct shoe should be as light as is compatible with the strength required to protect the foot during reasonable wear.

▪ REMEDIAL SHOEING

Heartbar and eggbar shoes are intended for clinical use only, to assist conditions such as laminitis; they should never be used on active riding horses because they can cause serious lameness, and could prove dangerous to both horses and riders because of the risk of slipping.

Horses with flat soles require skilled and careful shoeing to avoid foot damage. When anti-concussive shoes are required, plastics are useful. The extent of the horse's useful life is dependent on pain-free riding.

Horses with excessively low heels may need artificial elevation to prevent injury to tendons and ligaments. Special shoes can be made to alleviate the effects of heel collapse. Wedge-shaped pads may also provide adequate elevation.

Pads often serve a useful purpose in saving the sole from bruising. To an extent, they limit direct contact of the frog with the ground, though the nature of the pads, either leather or plastic, only has a minimal effect and horses seem to grip adequately while wearing them. A possible problem is canker due to preclusion of air. Also shoes with pads sometimes get sucked off when horses are ridden through deep mud, because of the manner in which they make ground contact. Some pads bear an imitation frog designed to stimulate natural expansion, and this overcomes some of the grip that is lost by having them there.

Eggbar shoe with studs to provide grip

A heartbar shoe is essentially used for clinical purposes and can cause slipping in ridden horses

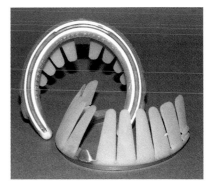

A plastic and aluminium shoe which can be glued into position without the need for nails

Four-Point Shoeing

We know from modern observation that the feet of horses in the wild
wear in a particular way, namely the predominant wear-points are four
in number, situated on the two heels and on the front of the foot to
each side, at the junction of the toe and quarter. This has led to a
system known as 'four-point shoeing', based on an effort to mimic the
natural – although there is reason to suggest that, by applying a shoe at
all, we are upsetting the rules of nature, and there is no room for
compromise when that is the case.

In fact this type of shoe leads to foot balance problems, and it also
predisposes to bruising, especially across the front where the receded
toe underlies the sensitive sole and may come in contact with it as the
shoe wears, and particularly when the weight of the horse descends on
it, as when landing from a jump.

In short, the move towards four-point shoeing needs to be assessed
objectively. It can be suggested that, once we decide to apply a shoe, the
whole of the hoof wall needs to give support in order to limit movement
and protect the sensitive sole. In the four-point system, the loss of
contact between the front of the hoof and the shoe is a weakness.

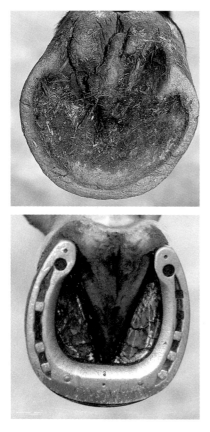

Four-point shoeing has its drawbacks and is
in need of objective assessment. It may be
that conditions in the wild, as demonstrated
by the unshod foot (*top*), are not directly
applicable to those in domestication

SUMMARY OF IMPORTANT SHOEING POINTS

- Have the feet trimmed and balanced by your farrier, taking full consideration of
  whole limb balance by monitoring movement before and after.

- It is important to gauge the proper angulation of the hoof with the ground, and
  ensure that the foot lands level in movement when the shoe is on; otherwise
  lameness may occur. Exceptions are only made where poor conformation demands it.

- Apply shoes that allow foot expansion and provide adequate grip for the surfaces
  your horse will be ridden on.

- Clean and care for your horse's feet with clockwork regularity.

- Ensure the diet allows for normal horn growth.

- Inspect shoe wear constantly, and never leave shoes on too long.

- Any shoe that prevents foot expansion or contact of the frog with the ground is
  likely to influence grip and cause discomfort that may even lead to muscular or back
  problems.

- Shoes that compromise grip should not be used on actively ridden horses, especially
  on fast or slippery surfaces, when they can put both horse and rider at risk.

Hoof Care and Hygiene

There are various routine precautions that may be taken in the day-to-day management of the horse's hooves. First, it is advisable to clean out the hooves every morning and evening, and before and after riding, to check for stones or damage, and to prevent infections such as canker. It is also important that the horse is kept in hygienic and dry conditions whilst he is stabled.

As the feet are a primary source of lameness, the horn requires good nutrition, including the provision of essential minerals needed for natural foot growth. Many people apply surface dressings, although there is in fact no evidence that they do anything to foster the natural health of the foot (equally there is none that they do any harm, either).

Horses left standing in the wet often suffer a general softening of the horn, which can lead to tenderness or infection. Conversely, modern riding horses left out on hard, dry ground without shoes will usually come in with cracked and often damaged feet; so they may need front shoes or tips while out. Heredity is certainly a factor in strong horn, though good feeding, and keeping a horse clean, healthy and disease free, are also critical.

Good grip is paramount when landing. Note also how the fetlock drops when bearing maximum weight

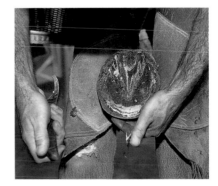

Foot balance starts with correct trimming

Large strongyles

Small strongyles

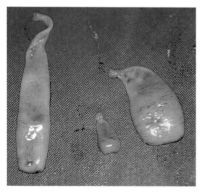

Tapeworm

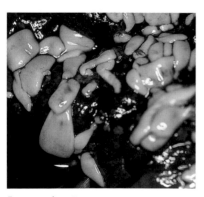

Tapeworm in gut

Worm Infestation and its Dangers

Equally important in the management of your horse or pony is a regular worming programme. The risk of worm infestation is decided by grazing conditions, horse densities, paddock size, as well as control methods, including those applied to limit ground contamination, such as rotational grazing and the removal of faeces, these picked up either mechanically or by hand.

Worm Types

The most important worm types are these:

- large redworms (large strongyles)
- small redworms (small strongyles)
- horse roundworm (*Parascaris*)
- threadworm (*Strongyloides*)
- hairworm (*Trichostrongylus*)

All these may occur in mixed infections, and all can cause disease in foals.

Next in importance are:

- tapeworms (*Anoplocephala* mainly, also *Taenia* and *Echinococcus* which infect cattle and sheep)
- bots (*Gastrophilus*)

Various problems are caused by the three worm types known as:

- pinworm (*Oxyuris*)
- lungworm (*Dictyocaulus*)
- liver fluke (*Fasciola*, infects cattle and sheep)

Lastly, there are worms that are quite common, but less significant clinically; these are:

- warble (*Hypoderma*)
- neck threadworm (*Onchocerca*)
- abdominal worm (*Setaria*)
- eyeworm (*Thelazia*)
- stomach worms (*Habronema* and *Draschia*)
- gullet worm (*Gonglyonema*)

large redworms	migrate through the blood vessels and cause potentially lethal colic, but are effectively controlled by drugs such as ivermectin.
small redworms	are prolific breeders. Most worrying is the fact that some are resistant to benzimidazole drugs; the larvae of some encyst in the wall of the bowel where they are inaccessible to most wormers; and the emerging larvae of both types contribute to spring pasture contamination, as well as condition loss and illness in affected horses.
horse roundworm	is a very large, white worm that produces particularly resistant eggs; it is more a problem in foals than adult horses. During their lifecycle they migrate through the body (which creates the possibility of insidious illness) before ending up in the gut to mature.
threadworm	is a common worm that infests foals in particular.
hairworm	is a common worm of both cattle and sheep and therefore to be considered when mixed grazing is practised, especially where routine worming is being avoided as part of a worm control policy.
tapeworms	are capable of being present in large numbers, and rising burdens may follow poor control measures. Pyrantel is the drug of choice and is effective when given according to the manufacturer's instructions in the autumn.
bot larvae	are large and can create heavy burdens in the stomach during autumn and winter; they are susceptible to ivermectins and preventive worming should be considered from the time flies disappear in autumn. Bot eggs are seen on the hairs of the limbs, particularly, in summer and can be removed, carefully, with a blade.
pinworm	the female lays her eggs in sticky clumps on the skin under the tail, where they fall off, or can be licked off from and so contaminate the stable or ground. They may also gain access to feed pots, or stick to walls and doors. This worm is controlled by most modern wormers, helped by good hygiene.
lungworms	donkeys are considered the natural host and horses become infected when grazing land contaminated by donkeys; coughing is a common feature. Fortunately the infection is effectively treated with ivermectin.
liver fluke	is primarily a parasite of cattle and sheep, common in areas of undrained land, there being a snail intermediate host: symptoms in horses include weight loss and anaemia. Oxyclozanide is an effective drug, though not licensed for use in horses; triclabendazole has also been used and appears to be non-toxic and effective, though this, too, is not licensed for horses. Do not use injectables unless it is with the manufacturer's recommendation, as some can cause serious reactions.
warble fly	has been controlled by eradication schemes in many countries, and is unusual now.
neck threadworm	is spread by a fly intermediate host; at present its clinical significance is not clear.
abdominal worm	is mostly a problem of warmer countries: it is seldom seen in temperate climates.
eyeworm	parasitises the tearducts and conjunctival sac and may need veterinary attention where it is seen.
stomach worm	larvae may infest open wounds, being deposited there by a fly intermediate host.
gullet worm	is considered to cause only minor local irritation.

SPRING

- The eggs of the horse roundworm and the hairworm may overwinter on pasture, as may some small redworm larvae, thus causing early grazing dangers.
- Large and small redworms that have survived within the host contribute to spring grass contamination.
- The threadworm is passed directly from the mare to her foal to begin new egg-laying generations at this time.
- Clearing faeces from paddocks provides year-round benefits and could be done weekly through the grazing season for maximum effect

SUMMER

- Mild, humid weather favours larval development.
- Where grazing areas have become divided into bare and rough patches, the latter provide cover for developing larvae.
- Strong sunshine kills many exposed larvae.
- Topping rough areas may expose larvae to the sun, though most infection stays close to ground level.
- The height of the fly season is marked by the appearance of bot eggs and sweet itch.
- Harrowing may in fact increase the risk of infestation by spreading contamination; therefore only harrow where a paddock can be rested.

AUTUMN

- Mature worms produce fewer eggs.
- Frosts kill off flies and many larvae.
- Most bot larvae reach the stomach by a month after the first frost.
- Heavily infested paddocks might be ploughed.
- Harrowing at this time of year might benefit those paddocks to be rested.

WINTER

- Stabled horses can be infected by horse roundworm, pinworm, threadworm and fluke.
- Liver fluke may stay infective on grass in mild, damp winters.
- Proper composting of manure kills most eggs and larvae, even the horse roundworm eggs.

The General Lifecycle of Worms

Horses most commonly become infested by worm eggs or larvae that are carried on the grass they eat. Exceptions include bots, where the eggs are deposited on the coat by the botfly and licked off by the horse. Some worms may penetrate the gut wall and migrate through blood vessels and tissues before returning to the gut to mature, creating the possibility of complications as they travel. Others do not migrate but spend their lives within the bowel, or, like the small strongyle, spend a time encysted in the wall of the gut, where they are protected from worming drugs.

Most worms lay eggs (or larvae) which are voided in the faeces, so continuing the cycle. Some require an intermediate host (such as liver fluke, and all of the last group that is described above, most of which are transmitted by flies).

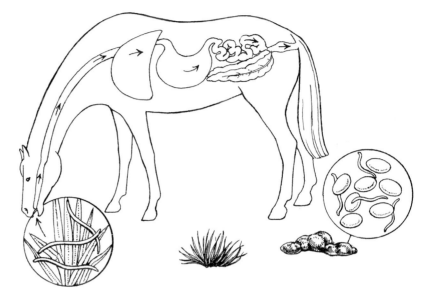

(*below*) Life-cycle of the typical roundworm. Larvae pass into the stomach and gut. Some migrate through the body but most return to the gut to migrate

CASE STUDY

There is a certain complacency about the significance of worms and owners very often are fooled into thinking it is enough to worm their horses every now and then with a modern wormer. They may not appreciate that different wormers are most effective against different worms and there is no such thing as blanket cover against all types. There is also the problem that surviving worms can set up new populations, and may even develop resistance to treatment. Also, freshly wormed horses can quickly pick up new burdens as there is generally no residual effect that will deal with these. You can't kill infective worms waiting on grass, you can only reduce their number by the kind of hygiene measures mentioned elsewhere in this chapter.

It is appreciated that paddocks become 'horse sick' by over-grazing. What this means is that there is an accumulation of worm eggs and larvae which makes the land dangerous to graze. An example of this was seen with a client who kept horses and gave them everything they needed without question. Unfortunately, the land was limited to less than twenty acres and, over the years, anti-worming measures had been inadequate. A good colt foal got an aneurysm and died, although it had been regularly wormed. A mare subsequently got recurrent colics and, while they didn't kill her, it had to be assumed they were worm related and that the cause was pasture contamination that could not be eliminated without ploughing and reseeding – a shame when the grasses were excellent and the fertility good. So there has to be pasture hygiene as well as intelligent worming in situations where grass is scarce.

Prevention

In intensive conditions, where the option exists, the removal of faeces
from the fields has been shown to significantly reduce worm burdens.
Manually it is a tedious exercise, though it may be vital on small
paddocks where worms are a problem and where drug resistance may
lead to a build-up of particular
worm types. Rotational grazing
with other animals is also
considered to be helpful, though
there is the possibility of cross-
contamination with worms that
parasitise horses, cattle and sheep,
such as fluke and the hairworm.

Routine worming may be
essential in intensive conditions,
as worm burdens will influence
health and affect performance.
But the accent needs to be on
hygiene, on avoidance, where
possible, rather than on a routine
of dosing that may fail in the face
of resistant worm types, and
management that doesn't think
beyond the fallibility of drugs.

As a general rule, we are
unaware of toxicity from most
wormers, though there are no
objective means of assessing their

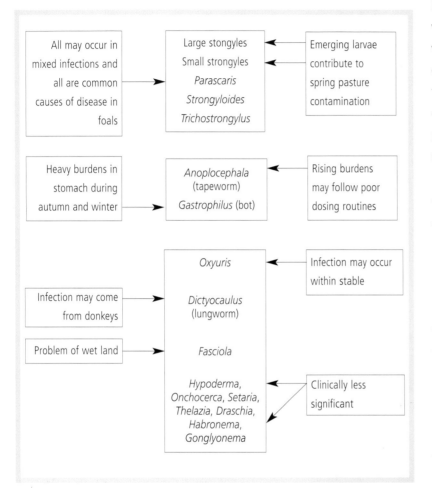

All may occur in mixed infections and all are common causes of disease in foals	Large stongyles Small strongyles *Parascaris* *Strongyloides* *Trichostrongylus*	Emerging larvae contribute to spring pasture contamination
Heavy burdens in stomach during autumn and winter	*Anoplocephala* (tapeworm) *Gastrophilus* (bot)	Rising burdens may follow poor dosing routines
Infection may come from donkeys Problem of wet land	*Oxyuris* *Dictyocaulus* (lungworm) *Fasciola* *Hypoderma, Onchocerca, Setaria, Thelazia, Draschia, Habronema, Gonglyonema*	Infection may occur within stable Clinically less significant

influence on performance in athletic horses.

Routine faecal sampling is also an important
exercise in any intensive situation, in order to assess
risk and keep a check on worm burdens. Horses still
die from worm infestations, despite the increased
effectiveness of modern wormers. It should be
understood that some worm types, such as
pinworms, threadworms and the horse roundworm,
may be transmitted within the stable, making stable
hygiene a very important matter. Liver fluke infection
may also be contracted by the horse eating hay that
has been taken from contaminated pastures.

Vaccination

Routine vaccination against influenza is an obligation for racehorses and many varieties of riding horse, including eventers and dressage horses, and any others over which there is an exercising central control body. It has to be surmised that the effect of obligatory vaccination has reduced the incidence of the disease, but there is little room for complacency, and equine flu is regularly diagnosed even in vaccinated horses, and the history and nature of the virus means it has to be constantly watched.

Flu is just one of many viruses that are capable of making horses sick, and its continuing prevalence is partly a reflection of the increased opportunities that increasing intensification offers to such organisms, and partly a reflection of poor management practices that often lower resistance to diseases of this nature. (See also Chapters 5 and 14.)

DIETARY CHANGE

Virtually all horses are subject to dietary change at some point in their lives, whether it is when they come in from the field after a spell off work, or when they change yards, or when they are away for a few days at, say, a show. As we shall see in Chapter 4, these changes have to be introduced slowly, and must be monitored constantly so as to pre-empt digestive upset and even more serious disease. As training progresses, quantities will be increased, but this has to be done according to energy requirements as well as body condition.

Grooming and Clipping

The reason for grooming is not simply to clean away surface dirt, but to stimulate the skin, to remove any material under which organisms such as ringworm might grow, and to unclog the pores in order to allow normal sweating.

The reason for clipping is to reduce the incidence of sweating in the ridden horse. It stands to reason that a horse will sweat more heavily if it is carrying a winter coat, which brings with it a number of problems: first, it will risk suffering the consequences of dehydration. Then there is the inevitable problem of drying it after it has been ridden, and the risk of its contracting chills and colds, especially if it is restricted to its stable when still wet from exercise. Horses not properly dried are more likely to

(*above*) Make sure your horse is fully dry before returning him to the stable after exercise

(*right*) Clipping helps to control sweating

(*left*) All worms are not seen on gross examination of dung

catch infection, and obviously, those with a thick woolly coat take a long time to dry without some form of help, perhaps heat lamps.

Finally, the whole process of getting a horse fit, and controlling its fluid balance and digestive efficiency, is made more difficult if it is not clipped.

Care of the Teeth

All horses need their teeth checked on a regular basis, every six months being the norm. Quite apart from the possibility of damaged, loose or infected teeth, a horse's teeth are growing the whole time, and even normal wear can result in sharp edges, especially on the molars; this can lead to quidding, indigestion, or even – and most seriously – refusal to eat. These sharp edges can be removed by a vet or recognised horse dentist using a variety of rasps.

In the process, any remaining crowns are removed, and any clinical condition, such as a rotten tooth, or of the mouth generally, is observed so that it can be appropriately treated.

Wolf teeth are nearly always removed, because no matter how small and innocuous they look, they frequently cause pain when in contact with the bit and make horses difficult to control.

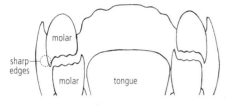

This section through the horse's mouth shows the wear of the molars which can result in sharp edges

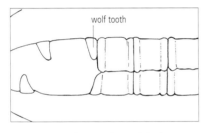

Wolf teeth are found in front of the first molar in the upper jaw

Tack

When a horse comes into work, careful thought must be given as to the tack it will need, that will be most suitable for the work it has to do.

Bits and Bridles

The purpose of using a bit is to permit adequate control over the horse to accomplish his work. There are many different types of bit to inhibit over-eagerness as well as truculence, but the bit selected should be the least restrictive compatible with the level of control required. When there are problems, such as the horse throwing his head about, first examine the mouth and teeth, or arrange for an experienced person to do this; if the teeth have sharp edges, or there are wolf teeth, these should be attended to.

If the bit in use is cutting the bars of the mouth, or bruising the gums, or causing the lips to bleed, it should be changed immediately. Always try a gentler bit, such as rubber or vulcanite, before changing to one that is more restrictive.

Neither bridle nor curb chain, if one is used, should chafe in any way: correct fitting of the bridle is of the utmost importance. It should

sit comfortably on the horse's head, and it should aid the prospect of control; if it pinches and rubs it can only invite resistance. Beware, too, the practice of an over-restrictive noseband: too tight and it can inhibit normal breathing, and even cause a horse to make an inspiratory noise (the same caution might apply to a too short standing martingale, since it encourages the horse to be over-bent).

If horses share a bridle, it is important to clean and disinfect certainly the bit between each one in order to minimise the risk of spreading infection.

(*above left*) Correct fit double bridle

(*above right top*) A bit that is too wide is likely to cause fewer problems than one that is too narrow, but is still incorrect

(*above right*) Correct fit

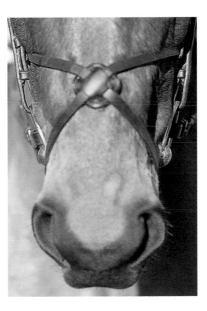

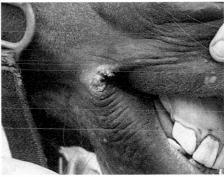

(*above*) Scarring from bit damage

(*left*) A bit that is too narrow will cause pinching and discomfort which will almost certainly result in resistance

Saddles

The purpose of the saddle is to carry the rider, and to distribute weight in a manner that protects the horse's back from injury. It is important that any saddle fits the horse properly: this means that the pommel should not make any contact with the withers; nor should there be any likelihood of the saddle pinching or rubbing anywhere, and so leading to sores; and the saddle should sit on the horse's back in such a way as to deflect the rider's weight off the spine.

(*right*) A poor riding technique might transfer weight unduly on to the spine with this saddle

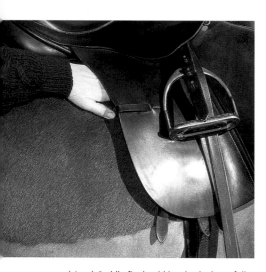

(*above*) Saddle fit should be checked carefully to ensure the saddle does not chafe or pinch at the back, or restrict shoulder movement at the front (*below*)

Neither the saddle nor the girth should restrict the movement of the shoulder or elbow, and the girth should not be over-tight, especially if non-elasticated; there should be no rubs or chafes as a result of bad fitting.

A common consequence of a badly fitting saddle is back trouble, just as it is often the result of poor riding techniques. Ungainly riders whose weight bumps down directly onto the horse's back, together with the effects of a poorly fitting saddle, can cause saddle galls, a situation that will almost certainly create pain, causing the horse to alter his posture in an effort to alleviate it; this may lead to lameness, which will only be relieved by fitting a proper saddle, as well as, possibly, manipulation. (See also Chapter 12, Daily Health Management.)

The significance of proper saddle fitting is only appreciated when there are problems. Chafes and galls are easily recognised and their cause understood. The horse probably won't be ridden again until the problem is resolved and an ill-fitting saddle is replaced, or some padding is introduced to prevent future rubbing.

There is less understanding of how saddle design, and poor riding techniques, influence back problems. Ideally, a rider will never come down heavily on the spine. Heavy riders, riding too short, have a tendency to rest on the back of the saddle; the horse's spine may need constant manipulation to relieve the pain this may cause. This influence is exaggerated as pace increases and jumping is required.

The lighter the rider, the better for the horse; the better the rider, the less weight is thrown onto the weaker part of the back. Except, very often, a heavy parent will exercise a horse for a student child who will only be home at weekends, or an enthusiastic owner will exercise horses to be ridden by lighter jockeys. The damage is done by the innocent, although ensuing problems are often attributed to the rigours of competition.

The type and fitting of the saddle is critical to the outcome and there is little disputing that longer leathers and a forward seat are more conducive to a horse's well being than a style that leaves the unfit with no option but to collapse on to the saddle when tiredness prevails.

These kinds of fault are what keep chiropractors, physiotherapists and vets in constant demand. They are a daily experience of my kind of work, although there are often diplomatic problems in explaining the cause!

Protective Equipment

If a horse is placed in any situation where it might strike into itself – such as when breaking it in, or when jumping – it is always advisable to protect the fore limbs. Tendon boots, bandages or other forms of limb protector may be applied to both front, and/or both hind cannons, and their design is important. Thus, the material used in any boots must be pliable, and should not cause skin irritation, or restrict the blood flow. Buckles and straps are to be avoided, as there is always a risk of doing them up too tightly; this can very readily cause the legs to fill, in a way similar to tendon injury – indeed, it is not impossible that some tendon injuries can be precipitated by boots that are too tight.

Velcro straps are the safest, because whilst a boot should never be too tight, it must also fit snugly and not come loose – straps or ties that can come loose may cause accidents and are best avoided.

Coronary band protectors help horses that are inclined to strike into their heels, and knee boots may protect those at risk of falling on roads – though restricting knee flexion is unwise: note that certain of these were designed as travelling boots, and were not intended to be used on ridden horses.

4 DIGESTIVE HEALTH and maintaining condition

The importance of the gut to a performing horse is in the simple and uncomplicated conversion of food from its raw state into breakdown products such as protein, carbohydrate and fat. These are needed for the production of energy in the quantities used in active riding, as well as for the maintenance and repair of body structures. Certain essential nutrients, such as some amino acids and vitamins, are manufactured in the gut itself by organisms that are critical to the digestive processes. Also, the gut must make available all the essential minerals and trace elements present in food, any of which are needed for ordinary, everyday activities, let alone the added demands of training and of intensive competition.

Good quality grasses can provide for all dietary needs but lush spring grasses may pose problems for laminitis sufferers

Digestion

Digestion is the process through which this conversion happens, while absorption is the means of transferring the then broken-down material across the gut wall into the blood, and thus to the body generally. The efficiency with which both these processes happen is dependent on the health of gut tissues, as well as on the well-being of resident organisms, and the presence of various digestive substances, such as enzymes. It also depends on the quality of the food provided and the ease with which it is digestible (adult horses, for example, may be unable to digest milk, which may cause diarrhoea when drunk).

Protein digestion is influenced by food source, by digestibility, and by the content of essential amino acids contained within it. Carbohydrate digestion is complicated on two fronts: first, those available from fibrous sources will depend on the condition of the fibre (whose digestibility reduces with the age of the plant, meaning that the nutritional value drops accordingly). Secondly, the readily available types present in lush spring grass are linked to the cause of laminitis, meaning these grasses are best avoided for at-risk animals.

Factors Affecting Metabolism

Any ingested substance which might adversely affect digestion can lead to illness: thus for instance, a diet of mainly bran (high in phosphorus) would upset the body calcium/phosphorus balance and could lead to bone abnormalities. There are many other factors capable of affecting metabolism in this way: for example, grasses containing oxalates inhibit calcium availability; excess dietary calcium can depress magnesium, manganese and iron absorption, due to competition at absorption sites; and diets that over-supply vitamin D can lead to toxicity and eventual death resulting from bone mineral mobilisation.

Toxins in food, too – be they infectious organisms in silage, or poisons such as ragwort baled in hay – are a potential hazard. All such details need to be accounted for so that the problems they bring can be avoided.

(*below*) Foal drinking from a natural water source, which must be free from contaminants if it is not to cause health problems

CASE STUDY A young horse was reported to be showing signs of lameness in both fore legs and, when examined, found to be heavy topped and over-anxious. He was a thoroughbred yearling colt being prepared for sales and his inexperienced owner had real trouble holding him for examination.

When standing at rest on concrete there was a constant trembling from the region of his knees, but he was in excellent condition.

Examination of his diet revealed he was getting too much bran, thus causing an imbalance of calcium to phosphorus, which had led to faulty bone formation and the anxiety might well have been caused by pain. Re-adjustment of the diet and a return to a correct calcium/phosphorus ratio led to resolution of the problem and the colt made his date with the sales.

Factors affecting absorption include:
- poor digestibility of raw materials;
- gut damage due to worms;
- ingestion of irritants that might affect the gut, such as heavy metals in water or acids produced as a result of local rock formations or acid rain.

Calcium absorption can be impeded by a variety of factors, such as excess phosphorus, inadequate vitamin D, incorrect pH, the presence of oxalates.

Absorption would also be affected by any clinical infection that damaged the bowel lining, perhaps leaving scar tissue in its wake.

The effects of absorption failure might include:
- weight loss;
- insufficient energy;
- metabolic diseases due to mineral deficiencies;
- bone abnormalities;
- the failure of body enzyme systems leading to conditions such as tying up.

PROTEIN TIPS

Manufactured feeds vary in protein levels from 8 per
cent (riding horses not competing) to 18 per cent
(foals, youngstock).

■ Use as low a protein level as is compatible with
body condition and work demands.

■ High levels may be justified for horses still
growing, that is up to four or five years.

■ Protein levels for competing horses have risen by
common use to more than 12 per cent, though
there is no evidence that such levels are beneficial
or necessary.

■ Feeding high protein levels, as well as causing a
horse to tie up, may contribute to more common
muscle tearing (see Chapter 10).

■ In the past, horses have performed to high
standards on a diet based on hay (protein 8 per
cent) and oats (8–12 per cent), with additions such
as carrots, apples and simple minerals.

■ Use protein supplements judiciously, and do not
be tempted to exceed recommendations; over-use is
known to increase body fat, and also to reduce
speed and exercise tolerance.

The Role of the Liver

The liver is an organ with many critical roles to play in the body. When a horse is performing well, we are unaware of its existence. In disease, however, it soon has an adverse influence, moreover its recovery is potentially slow, meaning that a horse with liver disease can be out of work for a long time.

The liver plays a central role in digestive metabolism and in the body defences against disease: it is responsible for the detoxification and removal of harmful substances in the blood; it is the store of some vitamins, also copper and iron; and it is the centre for the destruction of red cells, and for the formation of blood proteins as well as bile and lymph.

A functional liver is critical to any athletic performance in that it orchestrates normal metabolism at highly increased rates, and removes waste products quickly.

Liver disease is common in most infectious conditions, and also in poisoning; this causes an immediate loss of performance until repair is complete – which may take several months.

If you suspect liver problems, you should confer with your vet.

How Much Food?

As the horse's energy demands rise, the volume of food it requires will inevitably increase. The exact amounts depend on the horse's size and type, the volume of work he is expected to do, and on his individual metabolism; more pragmatically, it also depends on how well he can hold his condition under a heavy workload as well as perform to the best of his natural capacity against others.

Put simply, the diet must provide the following: enough energy for demanding exercise; protein to maintain body structures and repair damaged tissues; the basis of all essential vitamins and amino acids; and the minerals to create sound bones and sustain all the enzyme systems responsible for ongoing daily metabolism. Amounts may be increased as work increases, and reduced when the horse is having a break.

(*left*) Clipped horse in a stable showing good condition

It is not intended to go into complicated nutritional detail here, rather to look at essential facts that will act as quick reference pointers to what any rider needs to know.

PROTEINS

Proteins form 80 per cent of the body structure when fat and water are deducted. They are essential for tissue regeneration, the formation of cell walls, membranes, connective tissue, muscle, enzymes and hormones; they are also an essential element of blood. They consist of long chains of amino acids; some that are not available from dietary sources, are manufactured by organisms in the gut.

Feeding too much protein is wasteful, and can place a burden on the liver, especially in disease. The percentage of crude protein required in the diet of an active horse is 8–12 per cent; feeding above these levels increases cost, can be wasteful, and can precipitate tying up. Protein digestibility varies according to its source and the concentration in the diet. It is perhaps worthy of mention here that alfalfa hay may be as high as 18 per cent protein, and soyabean meal as high as 44 per cent.

Dried alfalfa

CARBOHYDRATES

All activities of the body require energy, and carbohydrate is the most common and immediate energy source, followed by fat and protein. In starvation, or when feeding is inadequate, energy is provided from body stores, which inevitably means weight loss. Simple sugars, such as glucose, provide immediate energy requirements and ensure that the heat needs of the body are catered for; it should be noted that horses kept in cold conditions burn extra energy to maintain body heat.

Lush grass can fatten ridden horses

Sugars come from dietary carbohydrate and are stored as glycogen for future use, as in muscle; any excess carbohydrate is converted to fat for storage. Most low fibre carbohydrates, as derived from grass or concentrates, are absorbed from the small bowel, thereby providing a quick energy source. Carbohydrates from fibrous sources are absorbed, following bacterial digestion, from the large bowel – and this means slower availability.

FATS

Fats are, essentially, the body's means of storing energy, and stored body fats are in a constant state of use and replacement. As training progresses, fat metabolism becomes more efficient and is able to provide energy more quickly. Dietary fats are absorbed from the small intestine, though some are later returned to the large bowel where they are altered by bacteria.

When feeding fat supplements, watch for interference with calcium metabolism, and conditions such as increased muscle tears and tying up. Horses and ponies that are too fat will almost invariably not be able to perform well.

Compound feed

It is important that laminitis susceptible animals be kept on bare paddocks or fully away from lush grasses

GENERAL FEEDING TIPS

- Each horse should be treated as an individual for dietary purposes.

- Any loss of weight will need a dietary assessment.

- Always look for causes other than diet, such as worms, infection or dehydration.

- Dehydration and electrolyte levels may be checked by blood sampling.

- Do not add more than a single mineral mixture without veterinary advice.

- Always look for quality constituents; do not feed spore-laden hay or badly saved grains; look for wholesome food materials, properly harvested and without any signs of degeneration.

- As excess carbohydrates are converted to fat, watch bodyweight in estimating quantities.

- Increase the amount of feed according to the horse's workload, as long as its bodyweight remains stable.

- Keep the diet as simple as possible: wide varieties of materials may ensure adequate source materials, but may complicate digestion.

HEALTH WARNING

In recent years we are advised of rising incidents of colic and inflammatory bowel conditions, especially ulcers. While the cause will never be straightforward, the move towards more complex diets seems to have come in strict parallel. Nothing is lost in keeping the diet simple, as long as the horse is holding its condition and performing to its best.

Strong bone comes from balanced mineral intake

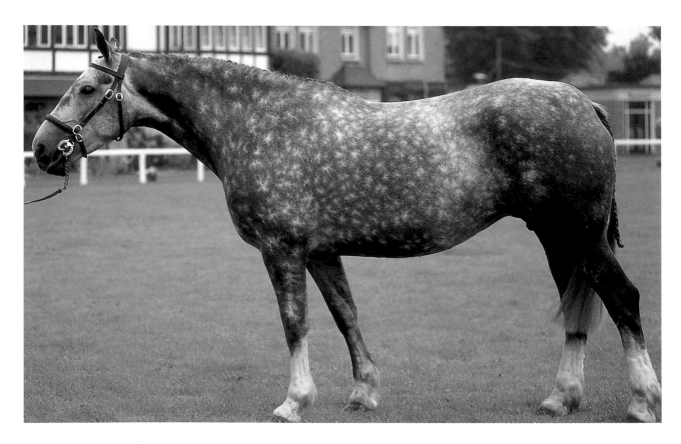

calcium and phosphorus	are the major structural elements of bone and cartilage, as well as being vital components of blood. Calcium is important to blood clotting and muscle contraction; phosphorus is essential to energy metabolism in cells. Both need vitamin D for absorption and metabolism; calcium is mainly absorbed in the small intestine, and phosphorus in the large.

The dietary ratios of calcium:phosphorus are 1:1 for adults, and 2:1 for growing or lactating animals. Conditions that indicate a deficiency include rickets, osteodystrophia and osteochondritis; also, tetany in long distance horses is associated with low blood calcium levels.

Calcium deficiency can occur through the feeding of a high phosphorus feed, such as bran, through absorption problems, or if there are oxalates in grass affecting availability. Phosphorus deficiency can occur in horses deprived of sunlight while stabled (due to interference with vitamin D metabolism); also in horses without the enzyme phytase to digest phytates, a dietary source of phosphorus present in many plants.

Grasses and other greens are rich in calcium; grains are rich in phosphorus. Calcium and phosphorus are available from meat and bone meal, dicalcium phosphate and numerous other supplements. |
| **magnesium** | is involved in many enzyme systems, such as those associated with muscle contraction; also in blood, soft tissues and bone. It is present in most feeds, though lucerne is a good source; however, absorption is hindered by high phosphorus and by oxalates in the diet. |
| **potassium and sodium** | potassium is involved in acid-base balance and in cellular enzyme systems to do with muscle contraction. Sodium is also involved in acid-base balance, osmotic regulation and nerve impulse transmission.

Hay is a good source of potassium, and grasses contain both potassium and sodium. Sodium is a constituent of common salt.

Deficiencies are uncommon, although persistent diarrhoea causes potassium loss. Spontaneous changes in blood potassium levels may follow strenuous exercise. |
| **chloride** | is an essential ingredient of gastric juice and bile; it plays a part in osmotic regulation and acid-base balance. Chloride is lost in sweat. It, too, is a constituent of common salt. |

(*from top*) Grass is a good source of calcium; bran is rich in phosporus; lucerne is a good source of magnesium; horses enjoying a salt lick

ELECTROLYTES

Sodium, potassium and chloride are all lost in sweat and need replacement. However, it is advisable to use specific electrolyte mixes specially balanced for horses; also, make sure that the electrolytes you use are absorbable, and use them only to effect. Ineffective preparations leave horses with dry coat and tight skin – besides, a balanced diet contains electrolytes, so there is only a need to supplement in specific situations; generally this would be when a fit horse has sweated heavily, say, in the course of a competition, or serious work, or during a race. Providing electrolytes above requirements is wasteful, and may even prove harmful.

PROPERTIES OF TRACE ELEMENTS

copper	deficiency can occur due to excess molybdenum in soil. It is marked by bone abnormalities and anaemia, and clinical problems need to be seen by a vet. It is normally adequate in the diet, but levels can be checked on blood analysis.
zinc	deficiency is associated with depressed growth, skin lesions and low blood levels on analysis; poisoning may occur from industrial pollution. Again, dietary sources are normally adequate.
manganese	is needed for cartilage formation; deficiencies are associated with poor limb growth and knuckling of joints. Pasture is a useful source.
iron	is essential for oxygen transport in the blood; deficiencies occur in heavy worm burdens. Most natural feeds are rich in iron.
fluorine	is present in bones and teeth; industrial contamination may result in an excess, and this might cause bone deformities. Certain rock phosphates are a rich source.
iodine	deficiencies occur in some areas, and one consequence of this is lowered exercise tolerance in horses with enlarged thyroid glands. Sea-salt and crushed seaweed are good sources, though beware of over-feeding iodine, as this could be toxic.
selenium	is deficient in certain areas. It is associated with 'white muscle disease' in foals and performance problems in adults, and it also causes greater susceptibility to infection; loss of hair, lameness, bone lesions and hoof deformities indicate toxicity. This is associated with plants that concentrate selenium, such as milk vetch and woody aster.
sulphur	is usually adequately provided for in dietary protein; NB over-supplying in pure form (eg flowers of sulphur) can cause death.
molybdenum	deficiency is associated with too much liming of the land, causing diarrhoea, weight loss and poor coat. It is present in most normal diets.
cobalt	is a constituent of vitamin B12; it is synthesised in the large bowel by gut organisms. Deficiencies are rare.

All vitamins play an active role in metabolism. Some are ingested in the diet, others are synthesised in the body, some by organisms in the gut, such as the water-soluble B vitamins and vitamin K. Good quality grasses provide the basis of an adequate vitamin source, though vitamin levels are affected by harvesting and storage. Good hay, oats, bran and carrots will provide adequate vitamins for stabled horses. Note that over-supplying vitamins can prove harmful.

vitamin A	Involved in disease resistance, bone formation, vision; it is present in carrots. Feeding too much can cause toxicity, although a large percentage is lost in curing and storing hay; deficiencies occur in horses fed only bad hay.
vitamin D	Essential to the metabolism of calcium and phosphorus, and to the formation of bone; it is synthesised in the skin on exposure to sunlight. Fish oils are a good source. Deficiencies may occur in stabled horses that receive no direct sunlight; excessive amounts can cause a gradual softening of bone and eventual death.
vitamin E	Involved in the metabolism of muscles. Cereal grains, green plants and hay are good sources; however, it can be damaged during the storing, harvesting or crushing (of oats, for example) of these. Diets that are low in selenium and high in unsaturated fats could be deficient in this vitamin.
vitamin K	Involved in blood clotting. Hay and pasture are rich sources; it is also synthesised by gut organisms.
Thiamin (vitamin B1)	Involved in cell metabolism. It is available from brewer's yeast, cereal grains and hay. A deficiency causes anorexia and heart problems; it is a factor in bracken poisoning.
vitamin B12 (cyancobalamin)	Essential for the formation of red blood cells (RBCs). It is synthesised in the gut, and is not contained in any vegetable source. Some competing horses benefit from supplementation; deficiencies cause anaemia.
Riboflavin	Involved in energy metabolism. It is widely found in nature; deficiencies cause a rough coat and watery eyes.
Folic acid	Also involved in the formation of red cells, and also synthesised in the gut. A deficiency causes anaemia. Present in green forage legumes.
Biotin	Involved in carbon dioxide fixation and other metabolic processes. Universal in food, it is, nevertheless, often in an indigestible form. Maize, yeast and soya are good sources, as well as grass and clover. Hoof defects occur where there are deficiencies.
vitamin C (ascorbic acid)	Vital to healthy tissues and body defences. The horse can synthesise vitamin C in the liver, and greens and fresh fruits are useful sources. Deficiencies cause lowered resistance to infection. Do not supplement orally, as it is poorly absorbed from the gut.
niacin	Essential for carbohydrate metabolism. It is synthesised in the gut, and is also available in brewer's yeast; deficiencies are associated with skin conditions, and mouth ulcers in species other than the horse.
vitamin B6 (pyridoxine)	Needed for protein metabolism. Widely available in nature; deficiencies are unlikely in horses.
pantothenic acid	A constituent of all live tissues. Widely available in nature; deficiencies are thought to cause a poor coat and diarrhoea.
choline	Widely needed in metabolism. Synthesised in the gut, and thought unlikely to become deficient in horses.

PROPERTIES OF VITAMINS

The Importance of Fibre

Dietary fibre is essential for the mechanical stimulation of the bowel, necessary to move the broken-down food along as it is being digested. Bacterial activity, mainly in the large bowel, aids in the breakdown of fibre into digestible sugars; and protozoan organisms, which are larger than bacteria, are involved in protein breakdown.

The effect of fibre digestion is to provide an ongoing energy source, the horse being a trickle feeder whose natural instinct is to graze constantly except when on the move. Fibre also provides a valuable food source when more digestible grasses are unavailable, as would occur seasonally in the wild.

The degree to which effective digestion can be achieved from fibre depends on its quality, but the bacteria involved depend on fibre for their own nourishment, and quickly disappear from the scene when there is none. A sudden removal of fibre from the diet will cause a loss

MAINTAINING A HEALTHY GUT

There is a growing appreciation of the importance of a healthy flora of gut organisms to everyday digestion; furthermore the use of probiotics has become commonplace as an indication of better understanding. A healthy gut is critical for an athletic horse, and the earliest signs of trouble with these organisms are evident in changes in the faeces, which may become too sloppy or too firm. It is a part of daily management to observe their colour, consistency and quantity, and to quickly notice any hint of change. If the consistency is too sloppy, body fluid levels might be depressed. Signs of sticky mucus on dry dung balls could mean inflammation or constipation, creating the possibility of toxin production and lowered performance. Colour changes occur according to diet, but sudden changes occur in disease. Blood from a small bowel source will turn the faeces black; fresh blood means problems closer to the rectum. Excessively dry faeces will often precede impaction-type colics; sloppy green faeces often precede spasmodic colic. Always keep a careful watch for worms.

(*above*) Meadow and seed hay

(*left*) Horses in the wild depend for their diet on available materials and may travel widely to find food

of organisms, and subsequent food eaten will fail to be digested, one possible consequence of this being acute indigestion. Furthermore, lost organisms may be replaced by disease-causing bacteria, perhaps leading to diarrhoea.

Gut bacteria are responsible for the manufacture of some essential amino acids not present in food, and of a number of vitamins, such as vitamin B12 or vitamin K, mentioned already; deficiencies can occur with any loss of natural organisms.

Hay and Silage Quality

Dietary fibre has to be of good quality and in constant supply; normal levels vary from as low as 6 per cent for foals (because the gut is not developed for fibre digestion) to as high as 40 per cent for horses being used for hacking only.

The fibre content of alfalfa, clover or ryegrass hay varies from 20–30 per cent, while the crude protein varies from 10 per cent (ryegrass) to nearly 20 per cent for some sun-cured alfalfa hays cut in early bloom. Energy levels vary from 1.5 Mcal/kg for ryegrass, to 2.5 for alfalfa hay and for alsike clover (US National Research Council, 1989, *Nutrient Requirements of Horses*).

Silage, by comparison with hay, will have a lower fibre content, and protein and energy levels similar to high-class hays, as above, but generally higher than meadow hay; it may therefore be advisable to reduce the quantities fed, and to follow the basic precept of gauging consumption against body condition and work demands. Always try to allow for a minimal continuing fibre intake in order to sustain gut organisms and prevent the horse eating bedding. Be aware, however, that indigestible roughage leads to gas production, which will interfere with breathing; this is also a problem when horses eat straw or hay contaminated with spores.

Avoiding Digestive Upset

Problems of digestion may arise for several reasons: when a horse's diet changes (for example, when he comes in from the field); if he is fed too much or too little; if he is greedy and bolts his food; if he is stabled for long periods at a time. There are various measures, however, that can be taken to avoid digestive upset.

First, horses that gulp their food at worst may choke, and they will not produce enough saliva for the digestive process to be effective, and this will lead to indigestion and/or food wastage. To overcome this

Hay should only be acquired from a reputable maker to ensure high quality

CHANGING THE DIET

Horses brought in from a relatively long period of being at grass will, inevitably, experience a change in diet, and it is important to manage this so as to avoid digestive upset. The change from grass to hay and hard feed must allow for the basic needs of the animal, and the process of change must be gradual rather than abrupt; indeed, any change of food sources and materials should always be made gradually. Horses just in should be given only hay for the first few days, and should not be offered large buckets of hard feed immediately – this could really upset their digestive process. Also, all food substances should be of acceptable quality, well stored and clean of contaminants, and anything new introduced a little at a time: thus you should start with a basic diet, and add to this only gradually and according to the horse's workload, gauging his needs against his body condition and his body weight.

problem you can incorporate chaff to slow down the horse's speed of eating and to encourage normal chewing by the jaw teeth.

Regularly spaced feeds help to reduce the feeling of hunger that is experienced by those horses in training whose forage intake is much restricted. Even for these horses, however, long periods with no fibre intake at all should be avoided. A loss of appetite may arise from overfeeding combined with overwork.

SUMMARY OF AVOIDING FEEDING PROBLEMS

- Overfeeding causes fat deposition and weight gain, leading to loss of fitness.

- Exceeding the recommended protein levels causes wasteful conversion to fat, it can complicate liver function in disease, and may precipitate tying up.

- Using high protein supplements as whole feeds leads to muscular problems.

- Feeding poor quality carbohydrate leads to weight loss.

- Using high oil levels can affect calcium absorption and so lead to tying up.

- Inadequate fibre means dead organisms and a disturbed digestive process.

- Very coarse fibre will not be digested.

- Using too many minerals and supplements risks absorption problems and also deficiencies.

A Clean Gut

For generations, it was always part of the routine of bringing horses in to 'clean out' the gut with a purgative. But attitudes have changed, and many equine dietary advisers denounce the procedure today. However, this does not get away from the fact that the horse's gut is a voluminous organ which may harbour material capable of hindering digestion; in fact, in the interests of health, it would be better if it wasn't there.

The routine of regularly mashing horses with boiled linseed/bran, for example, has a beneficial effect and can help clear the bowel without purging. In preparation, the linseed must be boiled overnight as it can otherwise be toxic, and it is advisable to scald it with boiling water rather than pour on cold water and then boil the mixture.

Body Condition and Weight

The surest way to detect loss of condition is by regular weighing. However, probably only professional yards have access to scales, but measurements are a guide to body mass and can be sensitive to immediate changes. Commonly, two parameters are measured, one being a girth measurement, the other typically the length from the elbow to the point of the buttocks. It is critical of course that there is consistency in the taking of these, since the girth varies from withers to pelvis, and to be helpful, would always have to be measured from exactly the same point; this also applies to any length measurement.

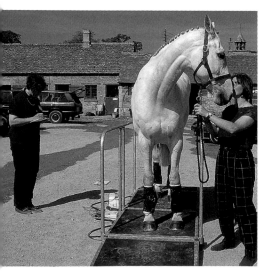

Regular weight checks can detect changes caused by diet or disease

A horse had constantly filling legs and was unable to work without blowing excessively. He lived in an area with sandy soil and clinical examination revealed little more than a raised resting heart rate and increased respirations without any indication of lung disease.

It was suspected that the condition was toxic and the horse was given Altan as a purgative. He was restricted to hay and water, all solid feed being held back. The effect was dramatic and within twenty-four hours he was purging excessively, though he never stopped eating and drinking. This lasted for three days before he dried up and the faeces returned to normal.

As drastic as were the effects of the purgative, the treatment proved effective. It has to be assumed that the cause was the sedimentation of sandy material in the large bowel, and the length of time the purging lasted was a reflection of the amount present. Such material will encourage the production of toxins due to interference with the normal gut flora and the result is a lowgrade poisoning of the whole system most commonly expressed by a loss of performance.

In investigating an outbreak of infection in a yard, attention came to the feedroom, even though the cause of the problem was attributed to a virus.

Associated symptoms of jaundice indicated there was liver involvement and many horses – there were over 100 – were moving badly and stiffened when worked, though not so badly they would be described as tying-up. It then materialised that the head lad, worried about the condition of his horses, had been feeding a 25% protein supplement as a whole feed, and most were unable to cope with this. After being rested for a few days, they would free out, but then stiffen again after work. The head lad refused to accept his feeding was at fault and it became necessary to use various subterfuges to get over the problem. Those that were put onto plain oats almost immediately recovered.

A client brought two mares home from stud with their foals and turned them into a field of lush grass which had been heavily fertilised. One of the mares was found dead the following day and the other was showing signs of profuse diarrhoea.

There being no time for tests, the surviving mare was treated with replacement fluids intravenously and drugs to stem the diarrhoea. She was cold to the touch and clearly deyhdrated but gradually responded to treatment and survived.

It has to be surmised that the condition was a form of colitis X, precipitated by the change onto lush from (possibly) bare stud pastures and the influence such changes had on the health of the organisms in the gut.

By multiplying the two figures, a result can be arrived at that parallels bodyweight. Any change would indicate weight loss or gain – although poor technique might ruin the exercise.

If digestion fails – that is, if the body does not get adequate energy, protein, minerals and so forth – a horse will not only lose weight and fail to perform, it may suffer clinical disease.

Responding to Weight Loss

If your horse is losing condition, the following measures should be taken:

- Ensure he is getting enough food for his work; assess his diet and the quality of each constituent, and ask your vet if you are still in doubt.
- Ensure that he is getting adequate electrolytes if he is sweating a lot in his work.
- Check for infection, worms and respiratory allergies.
- Pain will cause weight loss, particularly muscular, so check for this.
- Ensure the horse is warm, and is not burning off food in order to maintain body heat while in his stable.

FORMULA FOR FEEDING

- Stick to simple constituents of known origin, such as hay, oats, barley and bran, with additions of carrots, apples and a simple mineral mix, for example.

- Guage your horse's needs on the basis of his body condition.

- Do not adopt a routine of spooning in multiple additives, as the cumulative effect may be harmful.

- A simple diet may consist of good hay alone, depending on the type of horse and the amount of work; but never use bad hay.

- Good silage alone may provide more protein and more energy, depending on grass types, harvesting and storage; never use silage bales that have been punctured or contain evident contaminants, including fungi, dead rats or mice.

- Silage alone may not provide enough roughage; over-feeding it can make horses fat.

- The horse needs clean, digestible food materials, fed regularly in balanced form.

- A good fibre source should be available twenty-four hours a day.

- Do not overfeed, and use caution when introducing any new element.

- A clean water source is essential to meeting thirst requirements, free of chemicals including chlorine.

- Feed a weekly linseed mash.

- Prevent the eating of bedding.

Food Quality and Hygiene

Food for horses needs to be clean, wholesome, and free from any contaminant that might cause disease. The presence on hay of dust and spores frequently leads to respiratory disease and might lead to indigestion through disturbing the natural gut organisms. Contamination of food with rat urine could cause infections such as leptospirosis, a cause of jaundice due to liver damage.

It is clear that hygiene is important at every step of the horse's daily life, and although there are bound to be limitations in the varieties of food that will suit him, it is essential that whatever he is offered is of impeccable purity and quality. Make sure, too, that feeding utensils are clean at all points – this includes pots, buckets, sacks and storage bins: the risk inherent in contaminating food with dirt is the possibility of setting up infection. Think of nasal discharges spreading respiratory diseases such as flu and strangles, even on unclean hands, and the risk of transmitting worms, and other infections, too.

SUPERFICIAL SIGNS OF WEIGHT CHANGE
Performance may drop off in either case

Weight Loss	Overweight
Skin dry and tight	Well padded under the skin
Starey coat	Usually good coat with rich colour
Becoming thinner over the ribs	Ribs can't be felt
Neck is lighter	Prominent crest
Quarters and back less round	Excessively rounded quarters and back
Reduction in girth measurement	Increased girth

Quality of hay must be consistently high. It, or an alternative form of forage, will form the vast majority of the horse's daily intake

5 RESPIRATORY SYSTEM and infection

The importance of lungs to an athletic animal is in their ability to take in enough oxygen at varying levels of exercise to satisfy the body's needs, especially the demands from the muscle's when energy production rises towards the anaerobic state. The quantity of oxygen needed naturally increases with pace and effort. Also, the efficiency of gas exchange is influenced by disease and by management, and its understanding is therefore critical here; not in the way a scientist might need to know, but from a practical viewpoint of how to avoid trouble and ensure the best from your horse.

The horse fills his lungs when all four feet are in suspension at the canter

The Organs Involved in Breathing

Breathing at rest is a simple and undemanding procedure, as we all understand. Air is taken in through the nostrils and reaches the lungs by crossing the nasal passages, the pharynx, the larynx and the trachea.

The **pharynx** is a designated area at the back of the mouth across which food also passes on the way to the stomach.

The **larynx** is the voice box, and important because it is the site of several disease conditions that can impede airflow and generate abnormal noises during breathing, particularly as air is taken in. Such noises are a mark of flow restriction, caused most commonly by the vocal cord on the left side, which can protrude into the airflow as a result of paralysis and

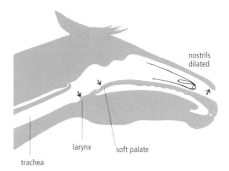

At the gallop, the horse's head is extended and the nostrils are dilated, allowing maximum airflow to the lungs. Note the streamlining of the soft palate, larynx and trachea

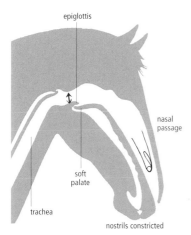

With the head in a flexed position, the size of the pharyngeal area (*arrowed*) is effectively narrowed. Here the nostrils are also in a resting state, limiting the amount of air intake

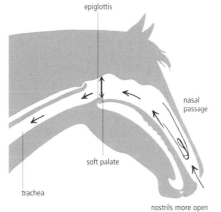

The nostrils will dilate as required in the sedentary animal, thus controlling the volume of air intake. The position of the horse's head has an obvious influence on airflow through the pharyngeal area (*arrowed*)

As more air is required, the nostrils dilate in an animal at rest suffering from respiratory disease. The horse's head may also be extended where the demand is great

Air travels (*as shown, right*) along the ventral nasal meatus, through the nasopharynx and larynx into the trachea. The mouth is closed off from the pharynx by the position of the soft palate in front of the epiglottis. In swallowing (*below*) backward movement of the tongue presses the epiglottis back to close off the larynx and lifts the soft palate to prevent entry of food material into the nasal passages protecting the respiratory system in both directions

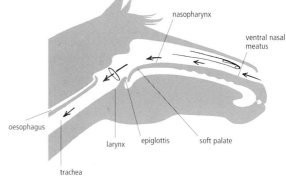

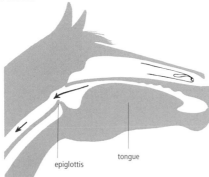

create the noise known as 'roaring'. There are a number of other conditions that can have the same, or similar, effects; but it is the reduction of oxygen intake that affects the horse, not the noise, and as we know, without enough oxygen, performance cannot reach its full potential.

The **trachea** is the windpipe connecting the larynx and lungs and placed at the front of the neck. Its surface membrane plays a significant part in removing dirt that gets into the system, including discharges that are generated through infection down in the lungs themselves. The effect of this is mostly evident at the nostrils, and explains many of the variety of nasal discharges that are often seen, be they the result of mechanical dirt (such as dust from shavings or dirty straw), pus from infections such as flu or strangles, or the watery discharges that are common in many bacterial or viral infections that attack different parts of the respiratory system.

At maximum exertion levels a horse may take 150 breaths per minute, or pro rata

How the Lungs Work

Within the chest cavity, the trachea divides and one section goes to each lung, after which the pathway further subdivides so that incoming air eventually comes in contact with a wide area of lung surface. Here, oxygen is transferred to the blood, and carbon dioxide is released so it can be removed from the body. This occurs across delicate membranes in minute areas called *alveoli*, and it is possible for these to be blocked by dirt and other foreign material (think of the dust inhaled when shaking out a dusty bale), or closed off on a wider basis, in infection or allergy. The alveoli are the working face of gas exchange, and their health and availability are critical to the expression of performance. If spread out like a sheet, they cover hundreds of square metres of ground surface.

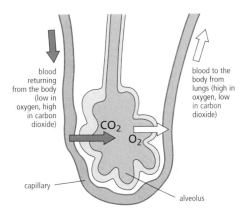

Gas exchange within the alveoli

The normal breathing cycle

Normal resting airflow	4 litres per second, which can be increased to as much as 75 litres in demanding exercise.
Resting breathing rate	In the region of 10–12 breaths per minute, including inhaling and exhaling. Can fall to as low as 8 or less in healthy, fit horses.
Breathing rate at gallop	Can be as high as 150 breaths per minute: this is equivalent to 2.5 breaths per second, or 2.5 strides, as the horse breathes in unison with its stride, exhaling as its feet hit the ground at the gallop, and filling its lungs between footfalls.

Signs of Disease

As the purpose of this chapter is to help recognise abnormality, it is important to deal only with signs that can be seen and understood. The objective is to learn the first moves away from normality, then to outline what can be done about reversing the situation.

The nature and depth of breathing at rest is a very good indicator of disease, as well as other detectable signs that can be recognised on close observation, as we shall see. It can be appreciated that even a 5 or 10 per cent reduction in available lung capacity during peak exercise will be hugely inhibiting: it will limit the animal's ability to express its full potential, and might even lead to internal bleeding as a result of the physical effort to find more oxygen. This, of course, would further

OBSERVING THE BREATHING RATE AT REST

- Effort is almost imperceptible.

- Long, steady intake and a pause between breaths (which disappears as the rate increases).

- No obvious use of abdominal muscles.

- Exhaling is a shorter part of the cycle, because there is less carbon dioxide eliminated than oxygen consumed.

- Ease of breathing is obvious to a vet listening with a stethoscope.

- A healthy horse uses only the lower, dependent parts of the lungs, a small percentage of total lung capacity.

- Upper areas are virtually silent, and this is normal – though such silence might be significant in infections where the breathing rate is increased, when the silent areas might signify pneumonia.

increase the horse's problems. At rest, a loss of 10 per cent capacity only means, perhaps, an added breath or two, but the difference can be critical when the horse is working. Such losses are marked by effort that can be observed while the horse is breathing at rest, and usually by some degree of abdominal breathing, marked by the contraction of the muscles on the floor of the abdomen.

Inevitably, if there is a resting breathing rate of 20/minute, the horse may have a temperature and be in need of your vet. That situation will be self-evident, though there is a need to be objective and to make sure the problem isn't caused by a lack of oxygen that is due to insufficient air circulation, for instance. But if a horse is dull and clearly off colour, then there is a need to get help quickly, because some infections are potentially lethal, and quick action might be needed to deal with them. So there is always that responsibility to decisive action, even if what we are interested in here are the less significant conditions that are not life-threatening, the influence

Any degree of lung disease may limit performance when the demand is high

WHEN THE BREATHING RATE INCREASES

There are various factors that might cause the horse's breathing rate at rest to increase; these might be:

- Temperature with infection.

- Temperature without infection (maybe after competing in heat).

- Tiredness after competition.

- Inadequate air in the stable.

- Stable too warm or humid, or horse too hot.

- Stable hygiene is bad; probably it will smell badly.

- The horse is suffering from allergic lung disease.

- Lung capacity is reduced due to previous disease.

- External stimuli are causing excitement.

- The acidity of the blood, perhaps due to lactic acid build-up.

- Pneumonia will cause horse to have a temperature, heavy breathing, and poor appetite – although clinical pneumonia is not common in adult horses now. Occurs more often in foals, where it is always serious, can sometimes be fatal, or leave permanent damage, so affecting future ability to perform.

- A bed wet with urine, along with inadequate ventilation, will increase the breathing rate because of a lack of oxygen and the presence of ammonia from the urine. The answer in such a case is not necessarily to increase the airflow, but rather to improve hygiene, or perhaps both on an interim basis, restoring a normal, clean, draught-free environment when the air has cleared.

- A vet can test lung health and capacity by judicious exercise, first having assessed the clinical fitness of the animal to undertake it.

- Assuming that all management factors are ideal, it is best to pass judgement on the breathing cycle when a horse is resting and there is no external activity that might precipitate excitement.

of which only interferes to a moderate degree with performance and the ability to express it freely and fully.

Inevitably, the time that lung disease becomes important is when it affects daily exercise as well as performance in competition. If your horse is subjected to a gradually increasing work volume, he will blow hard when his fitness is tested, and it is up to you to decide if the degree of this, and his recovery times, are within normal limits.

What to do about a Respiratory Noise

First, ensure that the noise is inspiratory – that it occurs when the horse is breathing in, and has its legs off the ground at the canter or gallop. If the horse's level of performance is satisfactory and he isn't becoming unduly tired in his work, ignore it.

If, however, his performance is affected, then there are several options. First, you could have a full clinical examination to make sure that the cause is not infection, dehydration or anaemia. If it is none of these, have a full respiratory examination, to include scoping.

If the cause of performance loss is definitely due to an operable lesion, such as vocal cord dysfunction or soft palate problems, then consider surgery. Do not, however, contemplate surgery where the cause is in doubt, particularly if there are infections present, or other clinical illnesses to be cleared up; even a change in training routine might be an alternative worth trying first.

ROUTINE HEALTH CHECK

■ Inspect the feed bowl and water container to evaluate appetite and thirst.

■ Check the horse's general demeanour and note any changes in attitude, his interest in external happenings, and his eagerness to go out.

■ Observe his breathing and count the rate at rest.

■ Take the resting pulse rate (see Chapter 7).

■ Check the membranes of the nose, eyes and mouth.

■ Check the lymph glands under the jaw.

■ If any of the above are abnormal, take the horse's temperature.

■ If raised, call the vet.

■ If normal, evaluate his energy levels and his responses when ridden.

OBSERVING THE BREATHING RATE AFTER EXERCISE

■ Horses that blow excessively and appear distressed should be examined by your vet as a routine.

■ If it is only a lack of fitness, as may happen after his first serious work, a race, or due to heavy or altering ground conditions, then the horse will recover and benefit in fitness.

■ If the problem is clinical it is a matter for urgent attention: for instance, he might be suffering from illness, and in particular infection, or from heart or lung disease; he might be anaemic, or lacking in oxygen (including at high altitudes); or he might be stressed if the weather is excessivly hot or humid.

Some of the conditions that might limit oxygen intake in the lungs are:

■ Inflammation due to infection.

■ Allergies caused, for example, by contaminated hay or straw.

■ Physical dust in shavings, paper, straw or hay.

■ Reduced lung space because of prior disease.

■ High altitude, where oxygen levels are lower anyway.

Evaluating Abnormal Changes and Discharges

In the Membranes

Owners generally don't look at the visible membranes because they are unsure of their significance, or of how to interpret what they see. It is nevertheless wise to take a regular look at the membranes of the eyes, nostrils and mouth, simply as a routine health check: this can help you to understand when there is, or is not, infection. Under normal circumstances and when the horse is in good health, these membranes are pale pink and show no indication of inflammation or aggravation – although a distinction has to be made between an inflamed eye membrane caused by a foreign body such as a piece of grit, when probably just one eye will be affected, and one caused by an infection coming from inside the body, in which case both eyes will be equally inflamed.

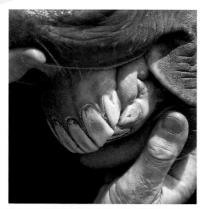

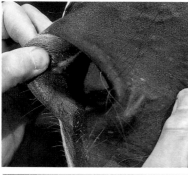

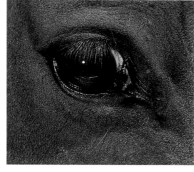

Checking the membranes of the mouth, nostril and eye will reveal changes in the horse's health. It is sensible to do this as part of a routine health check

READING THE MEMBRANES

■ A normal eye membrane is pale pink. A rich red colour is a sign of inflammation: it could be caused by infection, or by an irritant such as sand, hair, dust or a chemical.

■ Always check both eyes to eliminate localised infection, such as a foreign body. If both eyes are inflamed, systemic infection (viral or bacterial) is likely.

■ The nasal membranes are pale pink at rest and rich red immediately after work. Deviation from pink in the resting horse usually means infection: check lymph glands and breathing rate.

■ Jaundice is most easily recognised in the mouth and eye membranes: even the slightest hint in the eye may be significant.

■ Mouth membranes are often greeny-yellow from fresh grass.

■ Advanced jaundice causes a marked yellowing, also evident on the membranes of the vagina or sheath.

■ Anaemia is best seen in the mouth membrane, though advanced cases will also show in the eyes (there will also be a marked increase in heart rate and sounds).

■ Blue membranes occur in conditions such as nitrate poisoning when there is an interference with oxygen metabolism: this may occur as a consequence of drinking water with high nitrate levels.

IDENTIFYING DISCHARGES

Inflamed membranes can be accompanied by discharges which are watery or pustular in nature and might also be an indication of disease. Your vet can take samples and detect organisms present in discharges.

watery discharge	May appear on a very cold day and has no significance. In some viral conditions can be copious eg in equine herpesvirus (EHV) infection, when membranes show varying degrees of abnormal colouring and the horse might be constantly clearing its nostrils (though not coughing, as a rule).
purpling of eye membranes/ copious clear nasal discharge	Seen in cases of EHV-1. The nasal discharge contains the source of infection for other horses, which can be snorted out and carried on the wind for many miles.
pussy discharge	Infection. Most marked in strangles and secondary effect of flu.
nasal pus	May come from the sinuses, gutteral pouch or discharging abscesses on the affected side.
dirt in discharge	Dust in bedding, in the hay, or otherwise in the atmosphere.
pus in one eye	Normally a localised infection.

The degree to which colour might change in disease is variable, and in this, the eye and nose membranes are a better indicator than that of the mouth, where some discoloration might be due to food; for instance the pigments in fresh grass can have a tendency to mimic the appearance of jaundice. In equine viral arteritis (EVA), for example, the eye membranes become a very deep red, which is why the condition was once commonly referred to as 'pink eye'.

It should also be appreciated that nasal membranes are normally richly coloured immediately after exercise, so any assessment should not be made after work, but some hours later when all the horse's systems have returned to a state of rest.

The Lymph Glands

As a routine procedure in checking respiratory health, it is wise to inspect the lymph glands under the jaws as well as the membranes of the eyes, mouth and nose.

IDENTIFYING JAUNDICE AND ANAEMIA BY OBSERVATION OF THE MEMBRANES

Jaundice: In EHV-1, jaundice is associated with liver invasion, and the degree of discoloration, marked by slight yellowing of the eye membranes in particular, is mild when compared with the effect of something like ragwort poisoning, or leptospiral jaundice, when the membranes are much more markedly yellow.

Anaemia: All membranes become progressively white, although horses can be clinically anaemic with relatively normal colouring. The question is of degree, and although horses that are being asked to perform when they are only slightly anaemic are not clinically ill, they still might not perform well. The distinction is between illness that might be life-threatening, and one that only means a lack of fuel for demanding exercise when put to the effort.

The lymph glands act as a guide to infection in any area where they can be felt under the skin. This is because they are part of a whole body system fighting disease, and swollen glands usually indicate infection in the tissues they receive lymph from. In the head region, the manibular lymph glands are found under the lower jaw, at the back of the area between the jaw bones. They are not easily felt in normal, healthy, disease-free horses, but become very enlarged in conditions such as strangles, where swellings may grow to several inches across before bursting out and discharging pus.

Any enlargement, to the size of a pea or more, may indicate infection in local tissues, though glands can also be enlarged because of cancerous conditions though happily this is not common in healthy riding horses. The mandibular glands are commonly enlarged in many respiratory and chronic viral infections. While some horses may perform satisfactorily despite slightly enlarged glands, many do not, and the importance of these glands is as an indicator of health. Enlargement means some kind of irritation, usually infectious, and the horse is better off without any irritant rather than with one.

CASE STUDY

The common causes of anaemia are infection, worms, poisoning with substances like warfarin, etc but the condition can also arise from poor housing conditions when horses kept in cold buildings are obliged to use ingested energy as a heat source.

Anaemia is a common finding in redworm infection, but it is also a feature of liver fluke, which is less common, and eminently more difficult to diagnose. Diagnosis, in fact, is often only made in response to treatment as the horse is not a natural host for fluke and fluke eggs are not that readily found in equine faeces.

This situation was highlighted recently by a New Zealand farmer who was having trouble with his horses, while aware that deer grazing the same land were infested with fluke. The horses were performing badly and the situation had become so serious he was at his wits end. He was unable to get advice locally but contacted me to enquire about diagnosis and treatment. Following a conversation, he decided to treat the horses himself with an oral flukicide, even though the drug did not have any manufacturer's recommendations for use in horses. The danger was that the drug might prove toxic, but he felt he had no choice but to take a chance. Happily, treatment was successful. This is also quite a common occurrence here, especially in horses that have grazed fluke infested pastures, usually also grazed by cattle and/or sheep. These pastures usually have wet patches that do not dry out and are the habitat of the snail that acts as an intermediate host for liver fluke. Treatment of horses with flukicides is generally effective where there is infection, and incidents of toxicity are uncommon.

All places where horses meet are potential sources of infection

Enlargement is probably more common in bacterial than in viral conditions. The absence of swelling does not mean an animal is free of infection, but its presence is an indication of abnormality, even when a horse appears to be performing reasonably well.

Important Facts about Infection

Equine infections are so common now that most of us are aware of their effects. They are often unavoidable because the organisms concerned are so virulent; however, many can be prevented through knowledge of how they spread (see also Chapter 14).

Basically, infections are caused by either bacteria or viruses. Viruses are much smaller, and can only reproduce within living cells; generally they do not live for long outside a host, though there is variability, and some are more resistant than others – some can even survive boiling.

Bacteria are generally more resistant to external conditions, they live for longer periods outside a host, and do not need living cells in which to reproduce; an extreme example is the anthrax spore that can survive almost indefinitely in soil. Bacteria may attack tissues previously damaged by viruses, and this seems to be a regular occurrence in horses.

At the present time, viral diseases appear to be more common, though infection is a complex matter that is constantly changing. For example, mixed infections – that is, one virus or bacterium following on after another (or attacking together) – perpetuate infection, and the problem is not helped by management errors such as overcrowding or poor hygiene.

MANAGEMENT TO LIMIT INFECTION

- Identify any sick animal immediately, and provide elementary nursing care.

- Reduce exercise, and try to avoid any situation where a sick horse might break out in a sweat.

- Reduce the sick horse's diet if it is on a high level of feed, though ensure an adequate maintenance ration.

- Provide adequate warmth, and eliminate all draughts.

- Isolate sick horses as far as possible – though airborne infection should not be ruled out as a possibility.

- Attend and feed sick horses last.

- Keep a separate set of utensils for the sick horses, and do not use them for the healthy ones.

- Keep disinfectant footbaths outside the stables of infected horses.

- Wash your hands after dealing with infected horses.

- Be aware of the possibility of carrying infection on clothing, shoes and utensils: use a separate set of clothes, or overalls, that you can change into/out of.

- Avoid contact with 'outside' horses, and isolate any that come into a yard.

- Always seek veterinary advice where there is evident illness.

SIGNS OF SERIOUS INFECTION

- In **influenza**, the horse is depressed, off his food and will have a temperature.

- He may cough in the early stages of conditions like flu, which will probably be followed by a pustular discharge.

- Recovery is slow.

- **Strangles** may start with a sore throat, and the horse will soon be unable to swallow; he will develop swollen glands and discharging abscesses that seem to last for ever.

- **Herpesvirus** infection may start with abortion, or ridden horses may stagger and show slightly yellow membranes.

- In **viral arteritis** there is coughing, brick-red eye membranes and filling of the legs.

- Any infection will run its normal course: this may be only days with mild viruses, but recovery from flu or strangles takes much longer.

Infection spreads by direct contact between horses, by coughing within close areas, by coughing onto the wind, or by transport on the hands, on buckets, on grooming kit and/or on tack. It therefore goes without saying that it can be contacted at competitions, during transport, or when riding out through contact with horses in other yards or fields.

The distance an infection is carried on the wind will depend on prevailing conditions, and the size and weight of the particles: for instance, heavier discharges

won't normally travel as far. Birds may also carry infections, both mechanically and through any infection of their own systems (such as poultry with influenza).

In highly infectious conditions, especially when viruses have built up virulence in a close-knit population such as a studfarm or racing centre, airborne spread to neighbouring farms is a virtual certainty and happens as a regular occurrence. This doesn't mean that infections will have the same clinical effect in every yard, however, because this is often dictated by management factors, some of which favour disease, just as others don't.

Tiredness resulting from a long journey can make a horse vulnerable to infection, as well as widening the base of contact with other horses. Dehydration and exhaustion are other recognised causes, and there has been research in the human field that associates infection with excessive energy expenditure in endurance athletes.

How to Cope with Infection

The answer to low-grade infection is not necessarily found in drugs, but more commonly by tightening management and helping the horse to clear the infection through his own natural resistance. The best way of doing this is by giving his defensive mechanisms the chance to do their job as well as they can – and this would not be helped by a poor diet, the presence of worms, or lax hygiene.

It may be necessary to ease back on work, to critically assess the diet, and to provide an hour or two at grass. A most important factor in

Travel by air poses the risk of lowered resistance coupled with the possible spread of new infections

stabled horses is the provision of clean air and adequate warmth, and the elimination of draughts. This does not mean artificial heat, just enabling the horse to retain and maintain his own body heat, as well as simple, pragmatic procedures such as drying him properly when he is wet.

Some establishments may have infra-red lamps that they can use to help dry and warm horses after they come in, or on very cold nights; this has its benefits, as long as the heat is not used for so long that the stable becomes hot and stuffy, which can do as much harm as damp and cold. Even so, it is probably better for the horse to have a warm stable and few rugs, rather than be subjected to conditions that are so cold that all the rugs in the world fail to keep him comfortable.

The greatest mistake is to ignore sickness in a single animal that may then spread infection through all the others in a yard.

How Resistance is Lowered

A recognised aspect of modern infectious disease control is to consider the underlying causes of any outbreak, and to try to help a horse's recovery by eliminating them; certainly human medicine recognises this scenario. That is not to say that a virulent infection will be avoided by following stringent management recommendations; however, it might be suggested that poor management plays an important part in the establishment and spread of low-grade infections, and the whole question of understanding infectious disease might be greatly helped by a better appreciation of the links between the two.

FACTORS THAT LOWER RESISTANCE

■ The fact of being stabled, through restricting movement, adversely affects the horse's general circulation and body heat.

■ Horses that are kept in cold, draughty, damp conditions have to burn off energy to stay warm; their reaction to temperature change inhibits the immune system.

■ Poor hygiene will tend to cause a rank-smelling atmosphere, and this will irritate the respiratory tissues.

■ Improper or inadequate feeding will lead directly to deficiencies in the horse's system.

■ Worms and other parasites debilitate horses.

■ After infections of any kind, horses are susceptible to new organisms.

■ Overwork has a directly debilitating influence on the immune system.

■ Failing to dry a horse properly after exercise leaves it vulnerable to chills.

■ Long journeys may cause exhaustion and dehydration, and thereby lower immunity.

6 BLOOD and its importance in training

The blood is a living organ whose health and well-being are as vital to performance as is food quality and energy supply. It has a number of purposes, the main one being to supply all the horses body tissues with the constituents needed for life.

Blood is transported by the working of the heart, and it delivers its beneficial contents to the tissues via the arteries, then through a system of smaller vessels where it gives off its nutrients, after which it collects waste, such as carbon dioxide, and takes it back in the veins to the lungs, liver and kidneys, so it can be neutralised or eliminated fully from the body. It achieves all this by having fluid and cellular constituents, the fluid part creating the facility for transport. The cellular part is divided

The purpose of the circulatory system is the nourishment of all tissues and also the removal of all waste

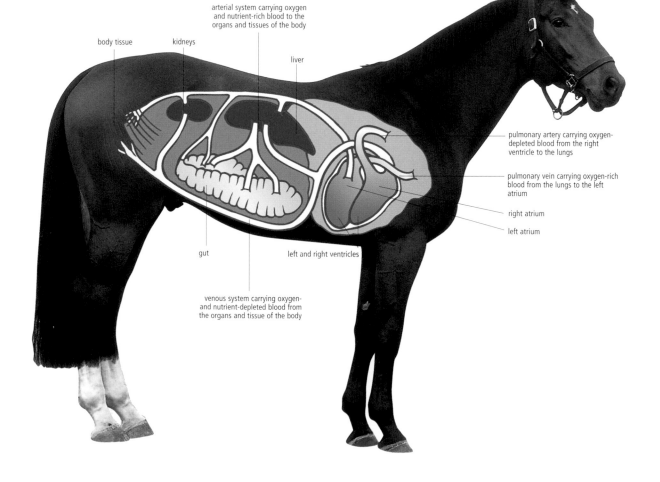

body tissue

kidneys

arterial system carrying oxygen and nutrient-rich blood to the organs and tissues of the body

liver

pulmonary artery carrying oxygen-depleted blood from the right ventricle to the lungs

pulmonary vein carrying oxygen-rich blood from the lungs to the left atrium

right atrium

left atrium

gut

left and right ventricles

venous system carrying oxygen- and nutrient-depleted blood from the organs and tissue of the body

The need for oxygen increases in demanding exercise

between red and white cells, the former being responsible for oxygen and carbon dioxide transport, the latter playing a critical part in body defences against disease.

The adaptation in the blood system as a whole to training is aimed at increasing tissue nourishment to facilitate better and more economic energy use, as well as improving the efficiency of waste removal. Just as we recognise that oxygen has to be supplied for energy production, the lactic acid resulting from anaerobic muscle use must also be effectively neutralised, or its influence on further effort will tell.

To understand how all this happens, it is necessary to consider some basic workings of the blood itself.

The Functions of Blood

The main functions of blood are to carry nutrients after absorption from the bowel directly to the liver, and then to the tissues generally; also to transport oxygen from the lungs to the tissues via the arteries, and remove carbon dioxide via the veins back to the lungs. It carries waste to the kidneys and liver for elimination or breakdown; and it helps to regulate body temperature. It reacts to training and exercise by stimulating the production of more red cells, and mobilising these as needed to increase oxygen transport. It responds to infection and trauma by mobilising white cells involved in defence and repair.

The most important of these functions when a horse is exercising is the quick and efficient supply of oxygen to the individual tissues involved in energy production; it must also remove the specific waste of this production, in order to neutralise acid resulting from anaerobic muscle contraction so that locomotion can carry on, even when at a reduced rate. We are familiar today with racehorses that collapse after racing if there isn't oxygen available in pure form.

The blood functions within a narrow range of acidity/alkalinity, known as the pH. This balance is most commonly disturbed by lactic acid production, though it can happen as a result of conditions such as diarrhoea, because of chronic fluid and electrolyte loss. The accumulation of high levels of lactic acid will cause pain in, and damage to, the muscles, thus ending the horse's effort.

Acidity due to lactic acid is in fact a normal physiological process, and is reversed without any need for treatment by ensuring that correct water and electrolyte balance are always maintained. Blood acidity, however, does reduce exercise tolerance and increase the breathing rate, and it may contribute to the initiation of 'tying up' in some circumstances (this condition is often markedly relieved by the administration of alkaline solution, to neutralise the acid, given intravenously by your vet).

THE CONSTITUENTS OF BLOOD

Blood consists of a fluid element, plasma, as well as the cellular element that, in the horse, makes up between 30 and 50 per cent of total blood volume. The cells are divided into red blood cells (RBCs), white blood cells (WBCs) and platelets. RBCs contain haemoglobin and are the transport vehicles of oxygen and carbon dioxide; WBCs help fight infection, repair damaged tissues and clear away foreign matter that gets into the body; platelets are cell-like structures involved in blood clotting, a critical function to prevent loss of blood from wounds. In this way they protect the vascular system, as well as the body as a whole, from the consequences of excessive blood loss.

■ RBCs

The total number of red cells dictates the quantity of oxygen capable of being carried, and any major reduction, as would be expected, is critical at exercise. One of the influences of training is to increase RBC numbers, as well as their capacity to carry oxygen; if there is a deficiency of either RBCs or their capacity to transport oxygen, performance suffers. It is worthy of note that horses kept in cold, poorly managed units where infection is rife frequently have low RBC counts over a wide number of animals. High figures could indicate fluid loss through dehydration; they could also indicate the possibility of drug use.

■ Haemoglobin

Haemoglobin is a protein contained in RBCs and intimately involved in oxygen transport as well as facilitating carbon dioxide return to the lungs. Arterial blood is bright red because its haemoglobin is saturated with oxygen; venous blood is darker because it has a lower oxygen content.

■ WBCs

Different types of white cells are recognised, each with a specific purpose; collectively WBCs form part of a complex system of body defences against infectious and allergic diseases, each with specific functions that come in response to specific tissue challenges. Blood analysis is an extremely involved area of medicine, and far beyond the remit of this book. Your veterinary surgeon will interpret results, and advise on action to be taken when disease is present. This may be relatively simple, as in the use of antibiotics to kill bacteria, or more complicated, as in virus diseases where the path to recovery may involve careful management, as much as therapeutic aids.

The Spleen

In horses the spleen is very important: it acts as a reservoir for RBCs, releasing while the horse is under the influence of exercise or excitement (explaining why blood results are high in excited or recently exercised horses), and being involved in the destruction of old RBCs. It also plays a part in the body's defences against disease.

The Lymphatic System

As well as being important in defending the body against disease, the lymphatic system plays an essential part in fluid regulation. We have already mentioned the lymph nodes and their significance as an indicator of infection, and there are many throughout the body whose function is to trap foreign matter, including organisms and cancer cells, and stop them from spreading to other tissues.

Anaemia

Anaemia occurs where there is a reduction in RBCs, or in the amount of haemoglobin within them; the influence of this on exercise is especially significant in competing animals. An anaemic horse will have very pale membranes and is likely to blow hard after exercise; there is an increase in heart rate and in the intensity of heart sounds. In severe cases RBC and haemoglobin levels will be significantly reduced.

Anaemia as seen in horses may be caused by one or more of several conditions: it is often a common expression of a heavy parasite burden, including liver fluke; it could also be a sequel to haemorrhage, either acute or chronic; it could result from deficiencies of iron, cobalt, folic

DEALING WITH ANAEMIA

- Ensure there are no worms by faecal sampling, and by dosing where necessary.

- Stop all fast work, do only steady canters, and not to the point of tiredness.

- Make sure that stables are warm enough by eliminating draughts, and ensure good floor insulation (even by using deeper, dry bedding).

- Check the quality of the feed, and allow a few hours at grass.

- Most greens contain available iron, so cut a green sod and put it in the stable.

- Supplement with injectable haematinics (ask your vet) of the nature of iron, B12 or folic acid, either individually (if known to be deficient), or as part of a combination, of which there are many available.

Horses subjected to cold conditions suffer more infections and are often anaemic

acid or vitamin B12; and it can also result from bacterial conditions (such as leptospirosis) or viral infections (such as equine infectious anaemia). Note, too, that RBC levels can become depressed under poor management conditions, so inducing a state of lowered immunity and, consequently, infection. Training also causes an increased destruction of RBCs as a natural turnover process: inevitably, if there is any problem with regeneration, anaemia can result.

For the athletic horse, any degree of anaemia is certainly significant.

DEALING WITH DEHYDRATION

■ All electrolytes lost in sweat are normal constituents of a balanced diet, and it is important to consider food quality and adequacy against exercise demands.

■ Chemicals such as chlorine in water often tend to have a diuretic effect, and cause an increase in urination; however, some chlorine evaporates if the water is allowed to stand (for up to 24 hours), though filtering may be necessary in extreme cases.

■ Rainwater is of dubious value as an alternative water source where there is any risk of pollutants.

■ Make sure your horse is clipped as much as might be needed to prevent him sweating unduly.

■ When your horse is stabled, ensure that he is neither too warm nor too cold: a cold stable with lots of rugs can cause energy burn-off; too much heat will cause sweating, especially under heavy rugs.

■ Use proprietary electrolyte formulae as needed, and judiciously; always use electrolytes after any profuse sweating, whether through work, stress or excitement.

Dehydration

Dehydration is the state that arises when the body loses more water than it takes in; this ultimately affects blood volume. At its extreme, dehydration is a serious aspect of disease conditions – we know how fluids are dripped into hospital patients in order to prevent the worst consequences, including death.

Under normal circumstances water is lost through urine, faeces, and from the lungs in exhaled breath. For the healthy athletic animal, the degree of dehydration is critical, and even small losses that are not rectified can interfere with performance. This mostly occurs as a result of sweating in work, although the problem is complicated by the loss of electrolytes (see also Chapter 4) that have to be replaced if fluid balance is to be restored.

Dehydration might also occur as a result of an infection that causes the horse's temperature to rise; or it might be caused by discreet sweating that goes unnoticed, perhaps when a stable is too warm or if the horse breaks out under its rugs (maybe after the stress of work). It could also result from improper feeding, from parasites, or even from drinking excessively chlorinated water (due to a diuretic effect).

The influence of dehydration on the heart can be very serious: by losing water, the blood automatically thickens, which means it circulates with more difficulty; its passage through capillary beds is therefore slower, and so the whole process of tissue oxygenation is then slowed down. As a consequence of this the heart has to pump harder, which has a direct influence on exercise reserves – the situation at its worst could undoubtedly endanger life.

The Effects of Dehydration

A 500kg horse has a body water content in the region of 350 litres. A normal horse can lose as much as 7kg of water while at grass on a mild day, and this can easily be doubled in an hour's work – this would be

Sweating before competing may result from excitement, but it could indicate disease

equivalent to 3 per cent of the horse's bodyweight. Any increase on this will lead progressively to tightening of the skin, sunken eyes and dry surface membranes.

As we have seen, sodium, potassium and chloride are all lost in sweat and have to be replaced in a balanced and readily absorbable formula. Horse sweat also contains as much as 15g of protein per litre, creating the thick and often soapy appearance seen; this is a possible source of insidious protein loss in horses that sweat consistently.

■ ELECTROLYTES

Racehorses and event horses often sweat excessively during their early training period, and for these, and also perhaps endurance horses, electrolyte replacement needs to be effective at least on a weekly basis. As training progresses, the amount of sweating reduces, and the fluid balance becomes more stable; electrolyte replacement can therefore be reduced, and used only before and after work, races and competitions. The best measure of effectiveness is in the horse's response to work and in the condition of his coat. Should he need excessive electrolyte supplements, speak to your vet.

Do not use formulae that have been prepared for use in other species.

Interpreting Change in Your Horse

At the point between illness and disease there are certain physical changes that may be observed in your horse:

- Loss of exercise capability: the horse may blow, or he may seem lifeless when ridden.

- In some situations, probably viral, a horse can be over-eager when ridden, but may sweat easily, and will quickly run out of energy.

- There may be a cough, he may be continually clearing his nose, and he may have a runny nose or eyes.

- He may be off-colour in the stable, inactive, and suffering a reduced appetite.

- Alternatively, he may become anxious and fretful.

- The membranes may become inflamed.

- The resting breathing rate may increase.

- The temperature may rise.

- The horse may feel cold to touch about the face and ears.

What to Do

- If the horse is off his food, has a temperature and looks unwell, get your vet. If he is none of these but just 'under par', cut back on exercise, do not do any fast work or jumping, and avoid making him sweat.

- Let him have an hour or two at grass to stimulate his circulation as well as his appetite. In the stable, eliminate draughts and make sure he is warm enough. Cut down his feed; a warm mash will help the digestive process. Electrolytes help with dehydration; they can also stimulate thirst, and the appetite, too.

- In well managed yards, recovery from most viruses is quick; this is not the case with bacterial infections, however, which may require antibiotics: your vet will examine and advise. When recovery is slow, use your common sense as regards exercise and training – in mild cases, when the horse is eating and drinking normally, it might be necessary just to ease back on training; but always be ready to seek advice.

- A week off work usually means a week to recover the same fitness, increasing accordingly with time missing from exercise.

- Never swim infected horses as a means of retaining fitness.

BIOCHEMICAL TESTS

A range of tests exists whose purpose is to detect variations in normal substances found in the blood. Thus, blood protein levels will provide an indication of nutritional status, as well as showing up losses arising from parasitic or other infectious diseases.

- **Enzyme tests** are used as an indication of muscle damage in tying up, although are perhaps not as useful as many riders might have imagined. Whilst there is a certain specificity, it has to be appreciated that the presence of any enzyme in clinically significant quantities only means that tissues that normally contain them have been damaged, and have released that enzyme. It does not necessarily indicate the cause, and it has to be said that there is a great deal of misinterpretation. While there is an undoubted increase in tying up today, many cases are misdiagnosed, and curtailing training programmes because of high muscle enzyme results is often the wrong advice, and can prove counter-productive when the problem lies somewhere else.

- **Blood chemistry tests,** of which a number are available, are used for indicating blood mineral levels where disease is suspected (think of calcium and phosphorus in bone development, for example). It is also possible to detect exposure to specific infections by measuring blood antibody levels (serology). These have become increasingly sophisticated, and nowadays results can be had almost instantly with regard to many important diseases.

Blood Sampling as a Guide to Fitness

Because of problems with diagnosis in disease conditions that often show very little outward symptoms, blood analysis has become a matter of routine management in many establishments where horse numbers are high. However, the benefits have to be weighed against the information provided as well as the cost involved, not forgetting the possible nuisance of blood collection in needle-shy horses.

In small yards the risk of infection is lower, and with good management, recovery is less protracted. Blood test changes do not act as a reliable guide to fitness, and are only a possible indication of already present, or impending, disease conditions. While some benefit may be had in larger yards when tests are used as a management tool, there are many imperfections, and it is perhaps worth considering that many successful yards operate without blood sampling even when clinical disease is evident.

Do you need Blood Tests?

For small, well managed yards there is little benefit in blood tests as a routine procedure unless there is a clinical problem – and even then, the results of bulk tests can be more confusing than they are informative, and possibly even misleading. Besides, horses don't like being needled, though many accommodate it; a lot depends on individual technique.

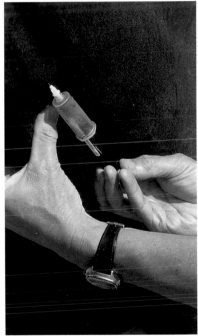

Collecting blood for analysis. Blood is collected by your vet from the jugular vein, using a sterile needle and special collection tube, under aseptic technique. It is important that the horse has not recently been exercised and is not in an excited state, as both can distort the blood picture; for the same reason using sedation is unsatisfactory. Early dispatch to the laboratory is necessary to prevent denaturing of the blood

At their best, blood results can indicate the early stages of infection. However, horses can be off form yet show no evidence in their blood, which can be frustrating. They can also be ready to do their best, yet have abnormal blood pictures, which might persuade their trainers not to compete them when, in fact, they might do very well (which has often happened).

A better system lies in good management, careful observation, and better horse expertise. Let your vet decide the need for blood tests, and interpret them against clinical findings when he examines a horse.

7 THE HEART and the ridden horse

We know more about the influence of the heart in athletic pursuits from education than from observation. As far as the horse is concerned, it is appreciated that a sound heart is critical to successful performance, although there is little general perception of the factors likely to facilitate heart action, any more than there is about those that might cause it problems. The good news is that the vast majority of horses have a functionally sound heart, and even of those that are rejected on vetting because of a suspect heart, many nevertheless remain effective pumping organs, and only a small number are so weak as to threaten the horse's life, or make it dangerous to ride.

Functions of the Heart

Put simply, the heart is a muscular organ that pumps blood through its four chambers. The purpose is to send oxygen-rich arterial blood to supply all body tissues so they can work and grow, and to take waste by way of the veins to the lungs, liver and kidneys so it can then be made safe or eliminated completely from the body.

The left side of the heart is more developed to allow for the greater pumping need of the general circulation over the lungs

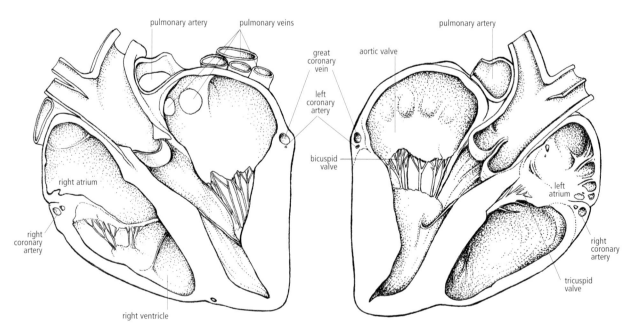

The Normal Heart

The heart is a muscular organ situated across the mid-line of the body, but mainly to the left in the chest cavity, and its beat is best heard just forward of the elbow on the ribcage of the left side. It has a special type of muscle that never tires because of the way its metabolism works, and this is critical to health: a heart that became stressed due to exercise demands would of course be useless, and thankfully only clinically abnormal ones suffer insufficiency.

There are four chambers divided by two valves, and two other valves on the main vessels that leave the heart (the aorta and the pulmonary artery); these all close and open as the heart pumps.

The heart has the capacity to quicken and slow as is required, and this capability is controlled both by the nervous system and by chemical messengers that come to it in the blood (for example adrenalin, released in states of fear and anger, stimulates the heart to quicken).

The Abnormal Heart

Probably the most commonly recognised abnormalities are murmurs. Heart murmurs in horses are very often less significant than thought, though they have an influence on value and will often end a sale; nevertheless, many horses with murmurs compete and race without any untoward effect, a particular case being Fort Leney, who won the Cheltenham Gold Cup despite having been previously rejected because of a murmur. There are two types of murmur, these being valvular and pericardial; and any other interference in the rhythm of the heart should also be investigated.

■ VALVULAR MURMURS

This type of murmur occurs when a valve loses its ability to close fully and there is a return of blood against the normal flow: the sound is like a 'swish' over the very defined normal heart sounds (mainly two, described as 'lubb' and 'dupp', because of their very distinct and positive sharpness); the 'swish' is created by the gush of the leaking blood.

Murmurs involving any of the four valves, though capable of being significant, are more often benign than performance-limiting, and once the heart can maintain a normal rhythm through an exercise session, it usually poses no risk. Inevitably there are exceptions to this, and you should seek specialist advice if you are in any doubt; furthermore it is advisable always to investigate where exercise tolerance is reduced, or a horse staggers or seems unduly stressed for the work it has done.

CRITICAL DATA

■ A resting heart contracts in the region of 40 times a minute in a healthy horse, though this figure may drop significantly with training, also with some illnesses.

■ In strenuous exercise, the heart may contract more than 200 times per minute.

■ The amount of blood pumped with each beat is about a litre.

■ The average output per minute is therefore about 30–40 litres.

■ The output may be six times as much at peak exercise levels.

■ Heart rates are higher in youth, disease, age and under the influence of flight, fright and fight.

■ The heart takes time to resume a proper resting rate after exercise, with a gradual reduction to less than 60 beats after ten minutes, and a full resting rate in fit horses (that haven't been exhausted) in an hour.

■ Very tired horses will have an increase over their normal resting rate for one or more days; dehydration may contribute to this, which is why it is important to provide electrolytes.

Valvular murmurs often result from infections and/or infestations; some are a consequence of protracted and serious lung disease.

■ PERICARDIAL MURMURS

Murmurs are also created by the presence of fluid in the sac known as the pericardium that surrounds the heart; they are serious because they increase the workload on the heart itself, and even if an animal is able to perform, it could easily be dangerous to ride. Pericardial murmurs are generally a result of infection involving the heart itself, and the presence of fluid in the heart sac creates the possibility of heart failure.

Clinically, infectious diseases directly affecting the heart appear to be on the increase, and almost certainly this is due to the changing face of equine viruses; happily most recover fully, though the progress of recovery needs to be carefully monitored by your vet.

■ RHYTHM INTERFERENCES

Any interference in the rhythm of the heart should never be taken lightly, and such interruptions are variable. Simple **dropped beats** that happen with regularity (say, one in every four) and disappear with exercise are generally not significant. Dropped beats that are irregular and persist through even mild exercise (such as a short trot) are mostly significant, and any such horse should never be ridden without advice from your vet.

Rhythmic problems may result from **disease of the heart itself**, though they can occur as **a result of chronic lung or liver disease**, due to the unremitting resistance this presents to blood flow.

Atrial fibrillation is a rhythm irregularity which is increasingly seen now; what it means is that the upper heart chamber is contracting independently, and randomly, of the lower, and it is always very serious, even putting the animal's life at risk. The good news is that it can be reversed – at least one such horse recently won a major championship race at Cheltenham. Fibrillation is sometimes a complication of viral infection, and may occur from working a horse either while ill, or too soon in the recovery period, or both.

This trace is from the heart of a horse with atrial fibrillation. The condition could be terminal, although this horse went on to win at the Cheltenham Festival. Note the virtual absence of contractions periodically

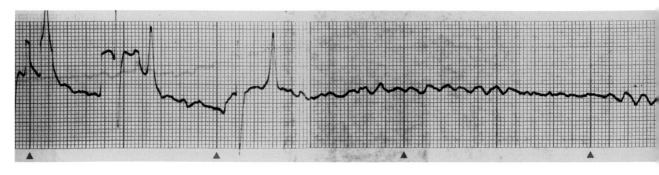

A yard of horses with suspected EHV-1 infection showed signs of mild jaundice. This is not unusual, as the virus is often found in the liver where it causes localised areas of damage. At a quick initial glance, these horses were fairly normal. They were eating, though perhaps one might have remarked that their coats were a bit dull, and that they looked marginally short of condition. Cantering on the gallops they lacked sparkle, but were not in any way distressed. However, when worked more seriously, some were definitely below par, and none was able to race until the jaundice disappeared and the infection was overcome – a matter of months rather than weeks, liver regeneration being slow after disease.

The effect on the heart was only a slight increase in the resting rate, which was not significant and couldn't be used as a basis for measuring well-being. With a stethoscope, the extra workload was marked by an increase in the volume of heart sounds, though this gradually reduced as horses recovered.

Factors that Affect the Normal Working of the Heart

The Blood

Aside from disease involving its own tissues, the heart is most directly affected by the blood, by the system of blood vessels and other organs referred to as the blood vascular system, then by the liver, lungs, kidneys and so on. In this it is also affected by any factor that demands an increased blood supply, either local or general, or that acts as a barrier to the natural flow; this might be caused by, for example, localised or whole-body **infections or injuries**.

The call for an increased heart workload is dictated by messages sent through the nervous system and blood, as already said. This is simple to understand: for example, a bad bruise is tense and painful due to an increased blood supply, and also as a result of resistance to throughput because of the swelling. The increase consists of extra blood brought to the scene in an effort to help repair, and blood that has leaked from the damaged tissues, thus often increasing local problems. Moreover chemical messengers from the injured tissue cause an increase in heart rate, and this lends to the throbbing effect. The resistance to flow can be compared to

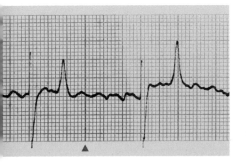

forcing water through a dirt-impregnated filter as opposed to a fresh one: the inevitable effect on the pump (the heart) is greater effort.

Similarly, disease in the lungs makes circulation of the blood through its vessels more difficult, and this may eventually damage the heart in chronic conditions where there is constant difficulty in breathing, such as with chronic broken wind (COPD).

Liver Damage

Likewise, though less easy to assess superficially, liver damage through **infection or poisoning** reacts on the heart. Normal metabolism (namely the generation of energy and the disposal of waste) is inhibited, and the damaged liver increases resistance to blood flow by being less permeable.

Worm Infestation

The heart is also likely to be affected by worm migrations, especially when clumps accumulate within the walls of blood vessels. This is a common feature in the life-cycle of strongyles, though the incidence has decreased with the advent of modern worming drugs, such as the ivermectins. Inevitably, where a blood vessel is fully blocked, the heart feels the effect and needs to work harder to try to overcome the obstruction. Where it doesn't, the effect is local tissue destruction and possible death, unless surgery can save the day.

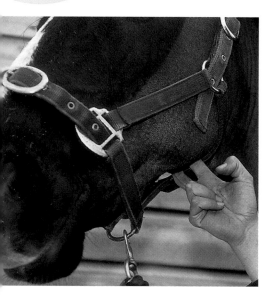

TAKING THE PULSE

This must be done methodically and on a daily basis, and always when the horse is rested and unexcited. Any change is a useful early indicator of training problems, perhaps disease.

- The easiest place to take it is under the jaw, on either side, about 4in forward from the angle of the jaw; the artery here has the feel of a small tube that rolls under the skin. First make sure that the horse is relaxed and rested, then fix the artery between the index and middle fingers, and feel the throb through the finger tips.

- Forty beats per minute (bpm) or less is about normal for a fit horse at rest, though some can normally be well below this. After exercise, the rate should reduce to less than sixty in ten minutes. A full return to resting rate should occur within an hour, depending on the work done and the state of fitness.

- Take the pulse as a routine under fixed conditions, for example morning or evening, in the stable when the horse is fully relaxed.

CASE STUDY A well known Irish race mare went to Galway races with a PCV of 33%. She had just changed ownership and was in good form working at home, though there was no time to try any treatment when the blood result arrived. The jockey was warned to be easy on her, not to stay up with the pace and to nurse her home. The yard, which was depending on her success, was on tenterhooks. However, the mare won easily. Subsequently, the jockey reported that she was beaten half a mile out, the ground being soft and taking its toll. But the others had gone too fast and all started fading. She just cantered on through them and finished going away, impressively. The celebrations lasted all night, especially as she paid thirty-three-to-one and there had been takers.

The Effects of Dehydration

After severe exercise, the body may have lost as much as 10–12 litres of water (based on a 500kg horse), or 3 per cent of its total body water. The effect on the heart is caused by thickening of the blood, and the greater difficulty, therefore, in pumping it through the vessels; if the dehydrated state is not relieved, a point comes when the heart may be subjected to severe stress, which could even precipitate death.

The Effects of Anaemia

Anaemia has the opposite effect on the blood to dehydration, though a similar effect on the heart, but for another reason. This is that the blood is thinner, therefore easier to pump, but an increased effort is needed to satisfy the tissue demand for oxygen, so increasing the heart rate. Put simply, a heart under pressure at rest will not be capable of producing peak performance in competition; therefore, monitoring the heart at rest is a good everyday indicator of performance capacity in any situation.

Recognising Heart Disease

Most abnormalities are detected by experienced clinical vets using a stethoscope. The opinion will either indicate that the horse can be ridden or it can't, or if there is a need for caution (in which case it would be rejected for sale). Where there is any degree of uncertainty, further tests can be carried out using electrocardiograms, ultrasonic scanning and other sophisticated technological equipment and tests. Your vet can arrange these, and will advise on the wisdom of doing so in a given case.

Using a Heart Monitor

Heart monitors are frequently used as a means of evaluating fitness on a daily basis throughout a training programme. Their greatest deficiency is the influence of undetected infection on performance, and the disappointment this brings to any formal methods of monitoring fitness or well-being when it exists unrecognised. As we have seen above, the changes may be marginal in low-grade disease, or even in normal physiological situations such as dehydration. The reality is that there is a point when performance deteriorates, and this may not relate to any recognisable parameter available from blood tests. Low-grade infection is all too common, and if it is undiagnosed, the influence on such a monitoring programme can clearly be very frustrating. The same applies to any method of gauging, or of predicting, performance capacity and is likely to remain so until better methods of diagnosing limiting, though nebulous, infections is found.

FACTORS THAT QUICKEN THE PULSE

- work
- excitement
- infection
- dehydration
- anaemia
- physical injury or pain
- stimulant drugs

FACTORS THAT SLOW THE PULSE

Some horses have a natural resting rate as low as 30 bpm, or less; however, a low rate may reflect dropped beats, and this should be checked with your vet – remembering that if the horse is working well and recovery is normal, there is unlikely to be anything wrong. Otherwise the pulse rate might be caused to slow:

- in some disease conditions, such as toxaemia, due to poisoning with bacterial or vegetable poisons;

- in the terminal stages of disease;

- by some forms of mineral supplementation, which may cause dropped beats that disappear on exercise and have no apparent clinical effect;

- in fibrillation, which may slow and weaken the pulse until it is almost imperceptible;

- by drugs used for therapeutic reasons.

Always check with your vet if there are major changes in the pulse rate without obvious reason.

DAILY RECORD CHART DURING TRAINING

NAME	Colour		Breed	Sex	Age	Height	
	SUNDAY	**MONDAY**	**TUESDAY**	**WEDNESDAY**	**THURSDAY**	**FRIDAY**	**SATURDAY**
Bedding	(eg straw/paper/shavings/special?)						
State of bed	(eg very wet and dirty/normal for conditions/smelly)						
Urine	(eg condition/colour/smell/quantity)						
Faeces	(eg normal/sloppy/hard/discoloured/too smelly/mucus present/change from previous)						
Comfort in stable	(eg warm/cold/damp/smelly)						
Morning: temp	0000000						
resting heart rate	0000						
respirations/min	000000						
Evening: temp	000000						
resting heart rate	0000						
respirations/min	000000						
Quantity of feed	(eg concentrates/hay/silage)						
Food eaten	(eg eaten/not at all/part)						
Water drunk	(eg normal/not enough/excessive)						
Weight	(000kg)						
Physical condition	(eg bright and well/slightly off colour/dull)						
Membranes	(eg normal/discoloured/yellow or bright red)						
Shoes	(eg wear/balance/need removing)						
When out	(eg interested and lively/slow and reluctant/sick or lame)						
Work	(eg length of warm-up/canters/work/jumping/in school)						
Movement	(eg in front of/behind/rider's comments)						

Observation and Daily Records

The sum effect of all this is that the best means of monitoring is by observation and recording daily data regarding well-being and progress in work; this will help you to trace trends and, looking back, see where problems started and ended, and where success began, and for how long it was maintained. In the competition horse – the endurance horse, the event horse, the point-to-pointer – to have a record of daily pulse rates is a useful guide to well-being and fitness; these should be taken at the same time, and always when the horse is at ease and rested (an example of such a chart may be seen on the page opposite).

Success in the past has always been based on acute observation and deep understanding, and failure often results from over-eagerness, from having the wrong priorities. For a horse to give of his best, he must be happy and well, not just trying to fulfil unachievable ambitions while perhaps even suffering pain.

SUMMARY OF IMPORTANT POINTS

- The importance of the heart in athletic horses is critical.

- Always have the heart checked before buying a horse.

- Many murmurs are transient and may be the effect of recent infections; many top class horses have prominent murmurs.

- Irregularities can be serious and may lead to insufficiency, which is risky; you may need a specialist opinion.

- The heart after work is a good guide to both health and fitness, when it has returned to a full resting rate.

- Heart rates reduce as the horse progresses in work.

- Monitoring rates is useful and should be gauged against the horse's degree of fitness.

- In almost any clinical infection, there will be a raised rate after work.

- Judging heart rates immediately after work can be unsatisfactory, and can miss the effects of mild infections.

- Heart sounds become louder in anaemia because of the extra work burden; the same occurs, for different reasons, in dehydration.

- Adopt a routine when checking heart rates, and be aware that any changing pattern may be clinically significant.

WHEN TO HAVE A HEART EXAMINED

- Any horse that becomes distressed or blows unduly after work should either have his workload reduced, or be investigated clinically, or both; the problem may not affect the heart, but the possibility exists and is too important to ignore. Horses that seem to become suddenly anxious or nervous may be reacting to circulatory insufficiency, and because of the possible danger to a rider, should have their hearts examined as part of a full clinical examination.

- Horses with chronic lung disease (such as COPD) should be examined regularly, as any such condition can cause heart problems.

- Horses should be examined after any viral disease.

- As a routine when returning to work after any serious illness.

- Older competition horses and hunters should be checked at the beginning of any new season.

- When buying a horse, its heart should be examined both at rest and after exercise; only complete a sale when you are assured as to its soundness.

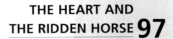

8 THE NERVOUS SYSTEM

This chapter investigates the role the nervous system has to play in the capability of the ridden horse, and the effects of damage or injury on its performance. The nervous system consists of the brain, the spinal cord, and the nerves that originate in these and that have various functions essential to life. The brain is in direct touch with every activity of the body, and is capable of intruding as needed to maintain body stasis, to react to external challenges, or respond to hunger, storm, drought and so on. The brain will tell a hungry horse to find food, just as it will tell him to put his back to the wind and rain, or to run when there are predators about.

All critical activities are subject to this central control, although there is delegation; movement in particular is mainly conducted at lower spinal level, through the means of what are known as reflex arcs. These work on the basis of sensors in tissues such as tendon or muscle that can trigger a reaction at the other end of a nerve circuit. They can work more simply in response to external stimuli. The easiest way you might

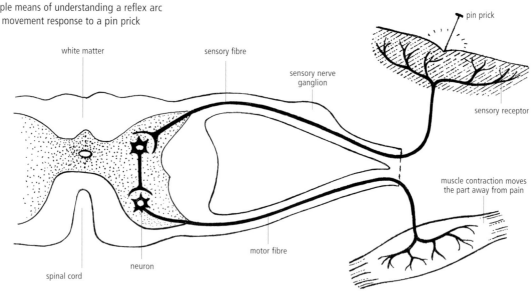

A simple means of understanding a reflex arc is the movement response to a pin prick

white matter

sensory fibre

sensory nerve ganglion

pin prick

sensory receptor

muscle contraction moves the part away from pain

motor fibre

neuron

spinal cord

understand this is to think of what happens when a horse is pricked with an injection needle: the sensation of pain causes it to move the challenged part away from the threat. This is an involuntary response caused by the sensation of pain, operating through cells at the level of the spinal cord; no message has to go to the brain, and the response is immediate and positive. The horse may then, as a result of thinking about it, decide to kick, run away or fight – but these are voluntary acts, now being dictated by the brain.

Reflex Arcs

The purpose of reflex arcs is to simplify the way the body works – if all forward movement had to be referred to the brain for clearance, progress would be very slow. It works in this way: the triggering of a sensor in one muscle will have a responding action in another, as muscles act together in movement; therefore the act of moving in any direction results from co-ordinated action in whole groups of muscles. This is facilitated by the reflex arcs, in that one limb triggers an automatic response in another – extend one of your own legs forwards and note the reaction of the other. In the horse, once the decision to move has been made, the hind limbs work together to push it forwards without any brain control; and the fore limbs must then respond in a controlled and co-ordinated way, not only to get out of the way of the forward-moving hind limbs, but to advance and make ground contact, and pick up and move forwards again as required.

The whole procedure is reflex until something happens, when the brain has to impose a decision that will alter the pattern of forward movement. For instance, an obstacle comes in the way and the horse has to stop, take avoiding action, or jump; then it continues forwards again, and the movement is once more reflex and without a need for conscious thought.

In the meantime the brain has the horse watching for dangers and impediments so it can impose itself at any time with the distinct purpose of preserving life and preventing injury.

Reflexes and the Paces

The sequence and co-ordination of the footfalls in the different paces – the lifting of the feet, their forward progression and then their placement on the ground – are all reflex in nature, and limb movement has to be controlled and rhythmic otherwise the horse would fall. At the walk, the sequence is a four-beat rhythm, at the

The brain is directly responsible for controlling a horse's reactions to danger

REASONS FOR LOSING REFLEXES INCLUDE:

- Nervous degeneration, as happens in human conditions such as Alzheimer's disease; there is an hereditary condition of Arab foals marked by loss of co-ordination; nervous degeneration is also a possible consequence of some deficiency diseases.

- From pressure within the spine in conditions such as wobbling, possibly also shivering and stringhalt.

- Some viral infections that attack the central nervous system, such as EHV 1 and viral encephalitis, seen in the USA.

- Toxic conditions such as tetanus, where the bacterial poison affects the nerves themselves.

- Any physical injury that might interfere with nervous conduction (such as a broken neck).

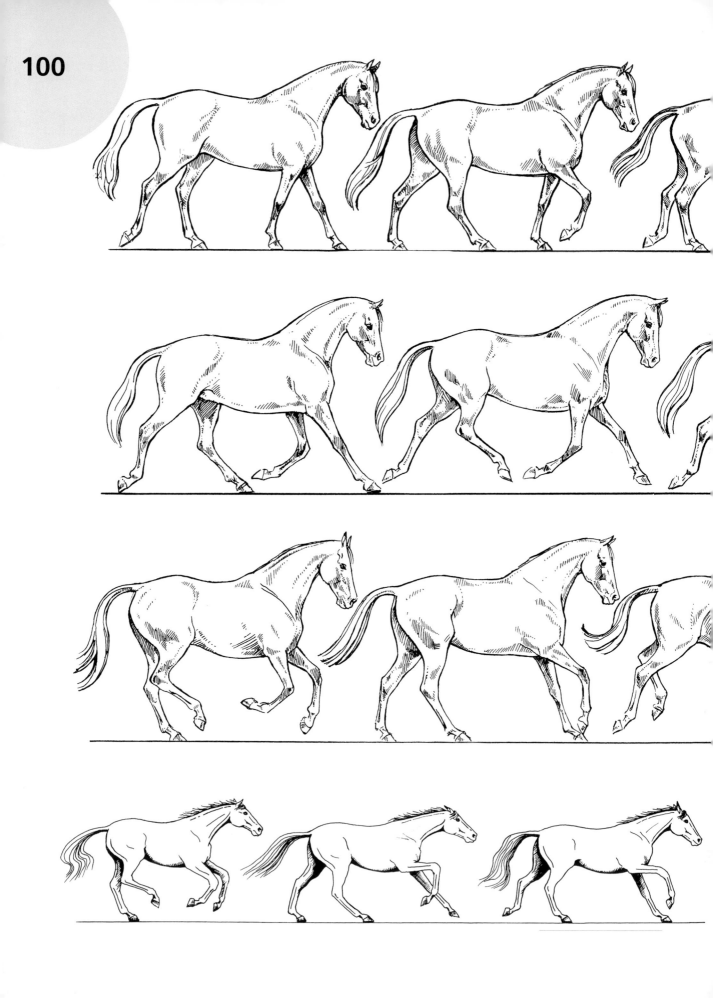

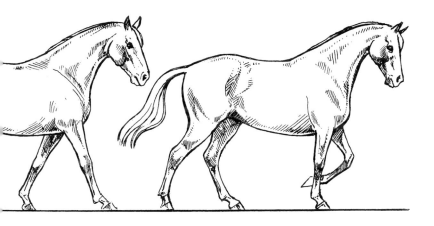

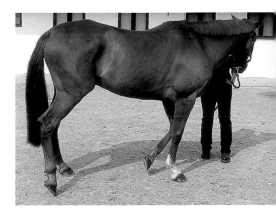

Abnormal movement like this may indicate
pain due to injury

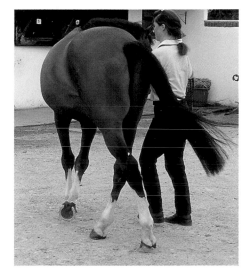

The ability to cross the legs over like this is an
important sign of normal reflexes in the related
nervous system

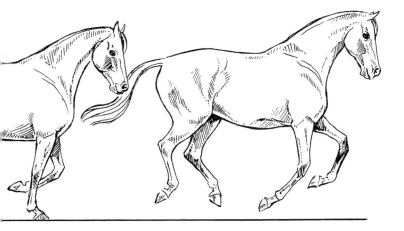

(*left from top*) The sequence of footfalls in
walk, trot, canter and gallop. Once the horse
has decided to change pace the control of
these sequences of footfall are delegated to
spinal reflexes

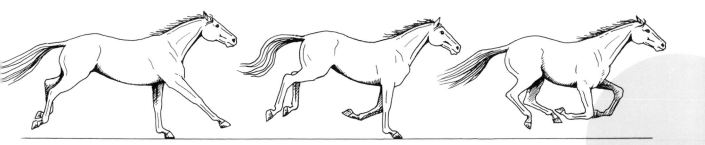

trot it changes from a four-beat to a two-beat rhythm, and the reflexes involved have to cater for this, tracking their messages in different circuits. The decision to change from walk to trot is made at the level of the brain, though the trot, once started, is delegated to the control of spinal reflexes until the brain needs to cut in again; the same of course applies to the canter and gallop. Thus the horse never has to think about where a limb is going to land, except when there is a risk of falling, slipping or crashing into an object – and when such risks arise, the brain is immediately in control, even if its attempted corrections are fruitless and the horse still comes to grief.

We would only note these reflexes by their absence, by the horse's inability to co-ordinate movement and follow the patterns we expect at every stage through the normal paces or in correcting errors; or should he not respond as we might expect, to a need for a sideways, backward or other complex reaction. The vet in a soundness examination is watching for the normality of these reflexes at all times, but particularly when the horse is asked to back, to turn on the spot, and in all stages of forward movement.

Righting Reflexes

The righting reflexes are those that help maintain the normal standing position and keep the head in an upright and balanced state. When a horse is pushed forcefully away from its resting position, its body will move away, but then return to a balanced position over which it has full control. This may involve stepping back from the direction of the push – but if there is any threatened loss of balance, it is able to correct it, and this is the effect of the reflex in action. The matter of balance is, of course, more complex, and the middle ear, the eye and the brain are all involved in sustaining balance through the complexities of jumping and competing.

Righting reflexes dictate the manner in which the feet are placed, and the whole nature of their contact with the ground: there isn't just contact, but sensation, and the control of the body's forward (or backward) progress. We have previously considered the matter of grip and slipping, and it is the presence of righting reflexes that dictates the compensatory efforts to balance the body when the feet can find no purchase, and forward impulsion is out of control.

Although this horse has made a mistake his ability to stay on his feet is a good indication of normality within the nervous system

The Importance of Righting Reflexes in the Ridden Horse

It is the proper functioning of these reflexes, in conjunction with directives straight from the brain, that allows a horse, after judging an obstruction, to stop, jump, swerve, slow or quicken, in order to avoid it. These are all voluntary acts, many of which are conducted through the pathways of spinal reflexes, after which the horse resumes normal reflex forward movement. Such reflexes are critical to speed, balance, jumping, or landing after a jump.

The brain will override them, however, when some external factor causes the horse to slip or lose grip, or threatens to cause him to fall: then the brain must dictate corrective action. The consequence of this type of situation is in fact very often injury, not just because the reflexes are overcome, but because control is often lost, and muscles and bones are subjected to stresses they were never designed to take.

Loss of Righting Reflexes

We most commonly see a loss of righting reflexes in conditions such as wobbling, shivering and stringhalt, the most serious being **wobbling**, when the horse progressively loses co-ordination and is incapable of controlled movement. The effect is obvious, and while the horse may be able to graze and amble about, the loss of control increases as the movement quickens or becomes more complicated; such horses are never safe to ride or jump, no matter how slight their symptoms may be. Once diagnosed, this condition is an accepted reason for write-off by insurance companies.

The way the limb moves in stringhalt shows there is interference with the nerve supply

In **shivering**, an affected horse shows a reluctance or inability to back up: the tail rises and shows a spasmodic, shivering movement, and the horse has trouble raising the hind limbs to place them backwards – and these show a shivering effect, too. It is not able to make a full backward stride with any ease, and the whole process is stiff, ineffective and often objected to.

In **stringhalt**, a hind limb (or limbs) is lifted high, as if it were tied to a string and the horse were trying to free itself. The movement is not natural and therefore becomes obvious. However, this is not to be confused with horses lifting their feet high because of being on an insecure surface, such as loose gravel; a horse with stringhalt shows the symptoms on all surfaces and usually at all times.

In both shivering and stringhalt, horses are often capable of being ridden and of performing. However, it must be appreciated that any loss of reflex movement may have serious implications, and cause a horse to stumble or fall. Having said that, horses have been known to race with either condition, and the only problem may be shoeing, as some affected shiverers have problems standing on one leg while being shod and very often the strain on the farrier might mean they cannot be shod behind.

Confusion with Lameness

The loss of reflex responses must not be confused with the inability of a limb to progress through a normal stride because of pain or physical injury of any kind. In such a case, the apparent loss of normal movement is caused by protective mechanisms aimed at preventing further injury. The action is, to an extent, voluntary, although the sensation of pain is a local reflex that inhibits use of the injured area, even if the possibility exists of the brain overriding that reflex and causing the part to be used, although with the certainty of even greater pain.

The distinction is between lost reflexes that will not generally return (recovery from conditions such as tetanus being an exception), and intact reflexes that are operating as an aid to the repair and protection of injured tissues. From the viewpoint of the rider, it is important to recognise any abnormality of movement of this kind.

Reflexes may also be impeded through simple back problems, though these can generally be corrected by manipulation. The obvious reason is pain or interference with conduction along any related nerve trunk. When a horse fails to place its feet as normal, or if there is any inability to correct itself in jumping or landing, or any suspected interference with balance, the situation needs to be investigated and the problem to be diagnosed and corrected, if it can be.

The Autonomic Nervous System

The autonomic nervous system is a special system concerned with the control of internal functions, such as the beating of the heart, the breathing cycle and the movement of food through the gut. It is, quite evidently, critical to life, though its influences are complex and do not concern us directly here. Abnormalities are expressed in serious disease conditions such as grass sickness, that require veterinary attendance and are unlikely to be compatible with exercise and performance. However, it is important to the wider understanding of the horse to know its simpler purposes.

SIGNS OF LOST REFLEXES

- Failure to sustain balance in movement; extreme cases would be unable to stand, as in advanced tetanus.

- Over-rigid, or inadequate support as the legs bear weight – this is not easily demonstrated, but think of a horse whose legs crumble as he lands from a jump, not just because of pain but because of his inability to hold firmly. If the legs are too rigid, concussion is greatly increased, so the jar when landing from a jump might also precipitate a fall.

- Inability to place the feet where they should land (the most common cause would be lameness due to injury, though nerve damage could have the same effect; for example, a wobbler will stagger about like a drunken human).

- Trouble placing the feet when turning in a short circle; this may involve failure to cross the limbs over, or exaggerated movement that lacks obvious control.

- Unable to back, typically seen in shivering.

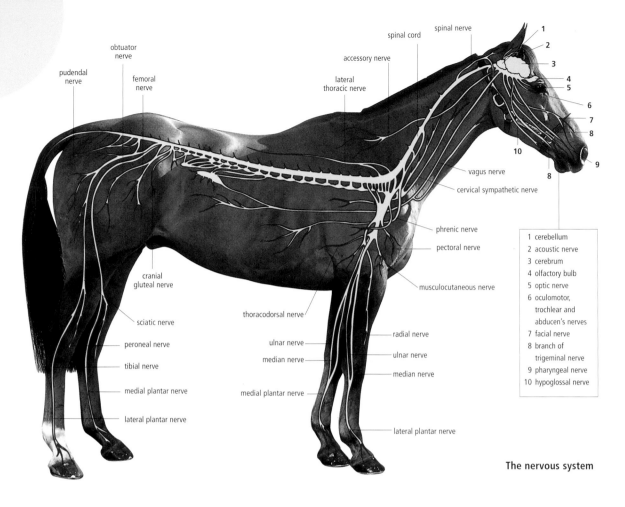

pudendal nerve

obtuator nerve

femoral nerve

spinal cord

accessory nerve

lateral thoracic nerve

spinal nerve

1
2
3
4
5
6
7
8
10
8
9

vagus nerve

cervical sympathetic nerve

phrenic nerve

pectoral nerve

musculocutaneous nerve

cranial gluteal nerve

thoracodorsal nerve

radial nerve

sciatic nerve

peroneal nerve

ulnar nerve

median nerve

ulnar nerve

median nerve

tibial nerve

medial plantar nerve

lateral plantar nerve

medial plantar nerve

lateral plantar nerve

1 cerebellum
2 acoustic nerve
3 cerebrum
4 olfactory bulb
5 optic nerve
6 oculomotor, trochlear and abducen's nerves
7 facial nerve
8 branch of trigeminal nerve
9 pharyngeal nerve
10 hypoglossal nerve

The nervous system

SOME FUNCTIONS OF THE AUTONOMIC NERVOUS SYSTEM

This system controls the following functions:

■ heart contraction, increasing and slowing the rate, dictating output;

■ respiration, to meet rising and falling oxygen demands, or to rid the body of excess carbon dioxide;

■ constriction or dilation of blood vessels generally to meet metabolic demands;

■ adjustment of the pupil for optimum vision;

■ bowel motility;

■ contraction and relaxation of the bladder, gall bladder, uterus, spleen;

■ secretion from glands such as the pancreas, adrenals, salivary glands, also sweat glands, tear production, nasal gland secretion;

■ metabolic processes in the liver, including glucose and fat metabolism.

Preparing the Body for Activity

Stretching Exercises

Among the reasons that human athletes do stretching exercises before a training session is to facilitate joint movement and stimulate muscle activity in order to create a gradual increase in metabolic activity, rather than shock the system by sudden forceful movements that may lead to injury.

In doing this, the muscles are stretched through static exercises that are intended to have counter-balancing effects across the reflex arcs: thus stretching of one muscle is matched by relaxation in another, or alternatively, tension in a corresponding muscle group in another limb.

The difficulty of successfully replicating these exercises in horses is immediately evident, and it has to be suggested that efforts to stretch equine muscles manually are often purely palliative. Think of trying to stretch a quarter muscle, the strength that would be needed, and the impossibility of co-operation from the average horse. A more natural way to achieve the same objective is to do adequate extended walking and trotting, either ridden or on a lunge rein; this procedure should be gentle at first, and requests for extension gradual, so that muscles, joints and nerves are brought to working warmth without risk and in an orderly and co-ordinated way.

The most practical form of stretching exercise for a horse is done by lungeing

Lungeing as a Stretching Exercise

Lungeing is a particularly useful exercise because, done properly, it allows for a gentle warm-up and encourages the horse to use muscles while on the turn that can remain unused in daily riding. Limbs that track short because of lameness become evident while turning, especially with the affected limb on the outside of the circle, since it is then being asked to stretch, and going short when failing to do so.

Lungeing on a good cushioned surface that provides plenty of grip is also useful for young horses being prepared for sales, when they are either unbroken or not yet ready to carry the weight of a rider. It is important that the ground surface be properly cambered and that there are no railings that might catch a leg and cause an accident.

When lungeing, ensure that the cavesson sits comfortably on the nasal bone and does not restrict breathing; also that the poll strap doesn't come in contact with the eye through being too loose.

Never allow a horse to be lunged on concrete. It is far too dangerous, especially with shoes on.

9 THE BACK AND BONY SKELETON

In this chapter we investigate the structure of the horse's back and the parts of his skeleton responsible for propulsion, and we will see how vulnerable they are to strain and injury; inevitably this would have a potentially catastrophic effect on performance. We will also see that chiropractic manipulation is an essential adjunct to soft tissue treatment if full normality of the horse's action, and therefore his ability, is to be restored.

The Spinal Column

The significance of the spine, particularly, in relation to soundness is increasingly recognised. There is expressed scepticism, even among some vets, that pain can be caused through, or lameness result from, the area of the spinal bones, the argument being: can the spinal bones move relative one to another so as to cause pain or impinge on movement? The answer, based on the number of horses being treated and the relief they evidently get, has to be in the affirmative. The perception of pain often starts with the rider, who notices a loss of impulsion, a changed action, or even a reluctance to go forward.

When humans suffer back pain, they go to a chiropractor, and the relief is often immediate and lasting. The same applies to the horse – though admittedly there is really no means of measuring or defining the effects, or of explaining the causes. Scientists don't like this, and are wholly sceptical because there are no signs that they can see or measure through technology, that they can quantify and record in their journals. Nevertheless manipulation has been shown to change gait patterns in at least one trial and whilst scientists quibble, horse owners are still left with the problem of an animal whose discomfort makes it reluctant to be ridden. They therefore seek resolution where they know it exists, and in a high percentage of cases quick success can often be expected.

Tracking short indicates lameness although the cause may have healed (eg a broken pelvis) and the horse may still perform

The considerable expansion in manipulative services, and the allied development of university efforts to teach manipulation within the confines of the lameness field, is a fair indication of the extent and reality of this particular problem. The incidence, it might be said, seems to have grown in recent years; although it may be just an increasing appreciation of this type of pain, how it inhibits movement, and how it may precipitate mulish behaviour.

Theoretical Reasons for Spinal Pain

There are several reasons why pain might be caused in the spine and associated areas; for instance, there might be untoward **pressure by bone on emerging spinal nerves**; or **bone may be touching bone** somewhere, the pain causing a muscular spasm that attempts to protect the area and prevent further movement. The same sort of muscular spasm may be caused as a result of spinal bones that **become wedged against each other**, in the same way that a drawer might get wedged.

Sub-luxation – a minor dislocation of spinal bones – is a possibility, although this is thought to be unlikely due to the anatomical nature of the equine spine. A much more frequent occurrence is **sprain of the lumbo-sacral junction**, possibly caused by jumping, and which causes acute pain when it happens.

Finally, spinal pain may be caused by **pathological lesions within the spinal canal** that cause direct pressure on the cord; these would be irreversible (as in wobbling and shivering).

The Incidence of Spinal Pain

The incidence of injury or strain to the spine is high in all ridden horses; inevitably it is more common in jumpers, though non-jumping horses – for instance, those that race on the Flat, endurance horses, gymkhana and polo ponies, dressage horses – also suffer, and virtually all types, however sedentary their existence, may show signs of back pain from time to time. Although problems can arise when horses roll or play when loose and free, the weight of a rider, as well as the demands of competition, especially when jumping, inevitably increase the likelihood of the type of sudden, uncontrolled movement that causes strain. Indeed, the incidence in all jumpers has to be close to 100 per cent in the course of an active athletic career.

While this may seem extreme, it includes horses that suffer minor incidents that are quickly relieved by manipulation and that never recur. Horses that are chronic sufferers are fewer in number, and usually

SIGNS OF SPINAL PAIN

- Stiffness and restriction of movement, especially in areas such as the neck.

- Tenderness to the touch over any specific area of the spine: this could be the neck, back, loins or quarters.

- Muscular spasm, detected manually in areas such as the loins.

- A tendency to dip the back when mounted (cold back).

- Altered stride length on affected side.

- May find backing difficult.

- Acute reactions in healthy related muscles when electrically stimulated.

- Problems with turning short, often finding foot placement difficult.

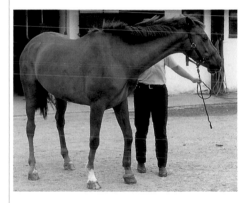

A horse showing difficulty in turning is expressing stiffness or pain, the cause of which will need to be investigated

present a complex injury picture that involves damage to structures elsewhere in the body, and also soft tissues; these can distort the anatomy in a way that places uneven (muscular) stresses on the spine when the horse moves. Most jumping yards find they need to use a chiropractor regularly, and most horses in these yards do need that attention, especially where they have made mistakes or fallen, be this in competition or training.

(*above left*) In landing the spine is influenced by concussion as well as the rider's weight

(*above right*) Balanced riding eases the loading on the spine as it bends

(*right*) Aside from the physical bruising here, the spine may be disrupted by both the abnormal bending as well as the effects of the impact

CASE STUDY

A well known point-to-pointer was referred for treatment because of suspected back problems. At considerable expense an unqualified manipulator was flown in to attend him, but failed to find anything wrong. The owner, a prominent figure in the horse world, was not satisfied with this, however, and the horse was sent back for physiotherapy. During the course of muscle stimulation in the saddle area, there was a sharp crack, and immediately the horse appeared to be freer in the way he moved: previously stiff and uncomfortable to ride, he changed, and from that day on was a pleasure to hack out and to train. He went on to win numerous races over the course of several seasons without apparent further problems.

The incidence of back problems is increasing and it is difficult to understand why so many horses being brought to sales are uneven behind and unsound from injuries in the pelvic region.

Some of the problems, thankfully, are easy to resolve.

WHAT HAPPENS WHEN A HORSE FALLS

- If a foreleg slips forwards, there is possible over-stretching of the flexors, and injuries would be most likely in, for example, the triceps, at the back of the shoulder.

- If a foreleg slips backwards, support is lost, and the horse may come down on that side, or extend the other foreleg in order to save itself.

- If a hind leg slips forwards, the muscles at the back of the thigh may be over-stretched.

- If a hind leg slips backwards, the muscles at the front of the stifle are most likely to take the strain.

- If a horse does the splits, the muscles on the upper pelvis are sometimes damaged, rather than on the inside of the leg; although this may be a result of trying to correct himself, or it may happen as the horse is getting up.

The regular strain on the back caused by mounting from the ground wihout assistance can cause injury

LIKELY CAUSES OF BACK PAIN

■ Jumping errors, and efforts made to correct or prevent them.

■ A rider's weight being quickly and forcefully transferred to the spine when losing balance, or being suddenly thrown back onto the saddle.

■ Abnormal use of the back muscles caused by excessive restraint of the head and neck because the rider is hanging on to the bit, especially when jumping.

■ Slipping up, falling, unco-ordinated movement.

■ Riding on surfaces that provide poor grip, leading to upper body tension and excessive muscular use.

■ Shoes that provide no grip, which has the same effect on the body as above.

■ Rolling and playing, either indoors or out.

■ A badly fitting saddle, combined with poor riding technique.

■ Injury to muscles directly influencing the spine.

The Likely Causes of Back Pain

In horses and humans, the immediate and obvious cause of any acute back pain can be strong physical effort, such as lifting (or pulling) weights. However, in people it can also be caused by poor posture or unsuitable chairs, and there is no reason to suppose that horses might not develop back pain for no apparent reason – indeed this frequently seems the case, in that the horse has not apparently suffered any untoward fall or injury, yet there is a definite change for the worse in both his action and his attitude.

Muscle Injury and Back Pain

Injuries affecting muscles that are directly linked to the spinal column have to be considered in any evaluation of back pain. The muscles and ligaments that are attached to, and act on, the spine are part of a whole unit, so it is only natural that, just as muscular spasm might result from altered relationships between bones, direct injury to spinal muscles can have an opposite effect. Ligaments, if they do become involved, appear to repair without complication, and do not often cause persistent discomfort once the muscles are treated and the bones have been successfully manipulated. But where an injury is primarily muscular, full recovery will not be attained by manipulation alone. Both these problems exist side by side as a regular occurrence, and both need to be corrected if there is not to be long-term and repeating trouble.

The situation may be further complicated by intensive training, as mentioned in Chapter 1. The more pressure we impose on our horses, the more injuries they risk sustaining, whether they are show jumpers, event horses, gymkhana ponies, polo ponies, even dressage horses: the faster, or more technical, or more complicated their work becomes, the greater the scope for error and/or strain. Horses slip, or fall, or perhaps we make them work for too long at a stretch, or they may even try too hard for us – and then they risk getting injured.

Investigating the Spinal Structure

Considering the Neck

From a practical viewpoint, the greatest degree of spinal movement occurs in the neck: visualise the movement between the head and neck, the up-and-down and side-to-side capabilities used in everyday tasks such as eating and looking about. Consider how the seven bones must alter position relative to each other to allow a horse to scratch its flank with its teeth.

The neck is a very strong unit, but it is quite commonly injured when horses fall. Whilst the disruption can be complete and the animal may die, there are a great many lesser injuries that do respond to manipulation. The instinctive – or reflex – reaction of the brain is to minimise the risk to its most vulnerable part, by instructing body parts such as the shoulder or the limbs to take the force: in other words, parts that are less likely to threaten life. Muscles, as we shall see in Chapter 10, can be injured at the same time, and may well contribute to continuing lameness.

Because of the relationship of the body nerves to the spinal bones in the neck, it is appreciated that neck pain can unbalance a horse, and problems that may appear to be related to the back and pelvis are often a result of pain further up the spine, which has an effect on the lower

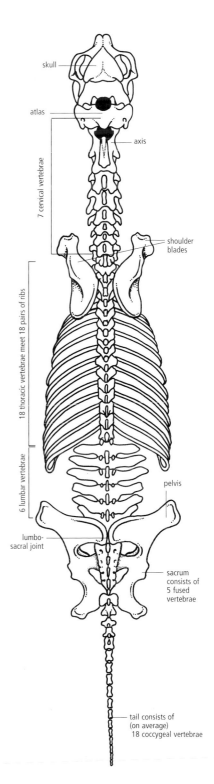

It is easy to appreciate how falls like this could disrupt the horse's spine

The atlas (**1**) and axis (**2**) shown from the
side (**A**), above (**B**) and below (**C**)

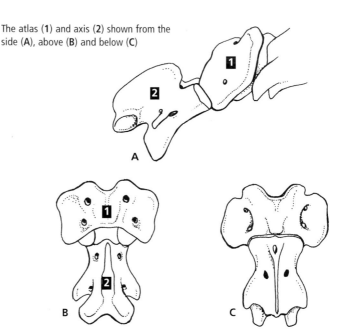

The weight of a rider falling suddenly on to
the back is a threat to the integrity of the
spine

structures. The reason is to do with changes in stance and attitude in
response to pain, and how these cause anatomical distortions; these are
most easily understood by comparing them with human back pain. Thus
an acute pain in the mid-thoracic region may induce the person to lean
towards (or away from) the pain, so causing curvature to one side and
tensions lower down the body; although these are often quickly relieved
when the original area is manipulated.

The Withers and Ribcage

The thoracic vertebrae are quite different in shape from those in the
neck: the bodies are shorter, and they have higher spines; and these are
particularly prominent in the wither area, and so are responsible for the
extra height here. The bodies are in close anatomical contact with one
another, and the fact that the ribs articulate between the vertebrae
adds a stability to this region that allows for very little movement.
However, because all these structures (18 vertebrae and 18 pairs of ribs)
are connected by soft tissue, there is scope for limited adjustment – and
because much acute back pain emanates from this region in humans, it
must be surmised that the horse is no different; indeed, experienced
manipulators confirm this, and certainly they improve horses that can be
seen to move badly before being treated.

This is also the area that bears the weight of the rider, at times in the
most extremely testing way, and it follows that a well fitting saddle is of
paramount importance. One of the purposes of the saddle, as we have
seen, is to distribute the rider's weight evenly, and divert it from coming
down directly on the spine; not just to avoid saddle sores, but to make

sure the weight is distributed over the ribcage, so easing the burden and avoiding direct trauma to the spine.

The Lumbar Region

The junction of the thoracic and lumbar vertebrae is situated at the back of the saddle area. The lumbar vertebrae are marked by shorter spines and wider transverse processes that give support to muscles vital to the stability and strength of this part of the back. The junction of the last lumbar vertebra with the sacrum is the main pivotal point through which the back arches when a horse jumps, which is why it is a point where injury is most likely to happen – indeed, this is a common finding. In fact the anatomy of this area is complex, and, as we shall see in Chapter 10, the dynamics of forceful forward movements, such as jumping, tend to lead to a more focused injury pattern, providing some indication of why problems are so common in this general area.

The lumbo–sacral junction is situated in a line close to the outer prominences of the pelvis, or the angles of the haunch. It is, as we have said, a weak point where strain is not uncommon, and it follows that horses suffering pain here are restricted in their movement: the area will be tender to touch, the muscles will show pain if electrically stimulated, and the horse will track short behind, possibly on both sides. In some horses the bony junction here, between the lumbar and sacral bones, may over time become ossified, meaning that they are less able to bend their backs; although once the process is completed and the joints are fused, the animal may perform without pain, even if moving less freely than before.

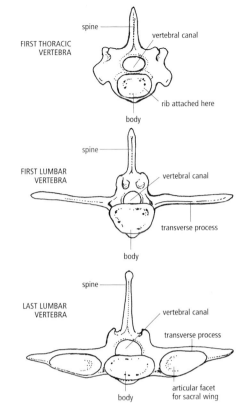

Vertebrae in cross-section

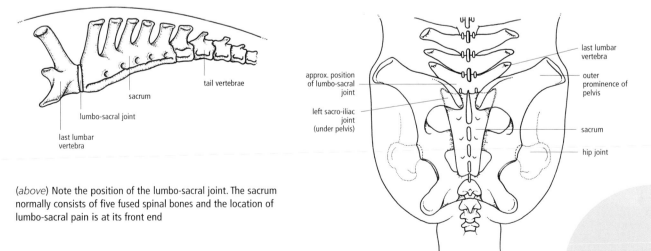

(*above*) Note the position of the lumbo-sacral joint. The sacrum normally consists of five fused spinal bones and the location of lumbo-sacral pain is at its front end

The Sacrum

The sacrum sits as a continuation of the spine and also as the roof of the pelvic canal, being bound into this position by a very strong array of ligaments and muscles. This area is critical because it provides purchase to the powerful muscles involved in hind-limb impulsion, and all its tissues are highly subject to disruption. Much is said about the influence of the sacro-iliac joint, which connects the sacrum to the pelvic bones on either side, but the weight of probabilities would suggest that soft tissues are the primary source of lameness in most injuries to this area. It is more than likely that loss of support, or pain through movement of the muscles and their attachments, is what causes most lameness here, although the picture is complicated by the influence this has on spinal bones. Manipulation is usually an essential adjunct to soft tissue treatment if full normality of the horse's action is to be restored, wasted muscles are to be built up, and working soundness achieved in what are very often long-standing, chronic conditions before they are submitted for treatment.

Injuries in the upper pelvic area are very common nowadays. They invariably lead to an altered gait, frequent wasting, and an upper line that is usually disproportionate when the horse is viewed from behind. The consequences are very serious for the future use of any horse.

The Tail

While the tail itself may be fractured and horses with bent tails are not that rare, the strength and functional normality of the tail is often a guide to injury or disease affecting the back and spine. In shivering, when the horse is backed, the tail lifts and shakes, indicating an influence on nerves supplying the area; similarly, any flaccidity suggests nerve damage. In racing, it is not unknown for injury to occur to the sacral attachments, when the tail gets bent back in a fall.

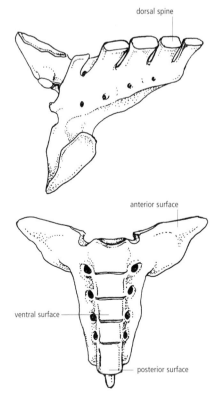

dorsal spine

anterior surface

ventral surface

posterior surface

The sacrum from the side (*top*) and from below

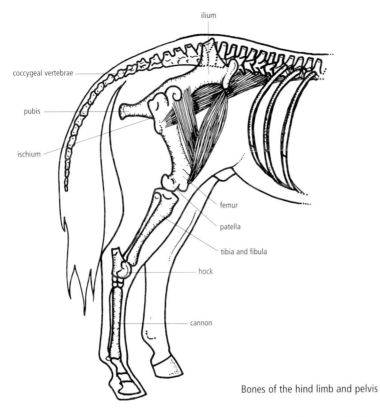

- ilium
- coccygeal vertebrae
- pubis
- ischium
- femur
- patella
- tibia and fibula
- hock
- cannon

Bones of the hind limb and pelvis

TIPS ON MANIPULATION

- Use only qualified equine manipulators: their training is an assurance of competence. It must be appreciated that this is a recent discipline, and will improve as the standard of knowledge and education develops.
- It can be suggested that manipulation is only effective on spinal structures, the bones, their joints and the emerging nerves; the clinical results of any other manipulative procedures have yet to be consistently proven beneficial.
- Most routine manipulation can be safely conducted without the use of sedatives.
- There are very limited indications for general anaesthesia in manipulating horses, and the results gained from un-anaesthetised horses compare more than favourably with those that are 'knocked out'.
- If a horse is jumping regularly, watch its action closely and get into the habit of gently feeling along the spine for pain resulting from light, finger-tip pressure. Sudden changes in reaction can be significant.
- Check, as far as you can, the horse's ability and willingness to move its neck through a full range of movements: for instance, touching its shoulder with its muzzle.
- Note any alterations in movement when riding, and compare the horse's action when led in hand without saddle or rider; if there is an obvious difference, seek advice or consult a chiropractor.
- Various types of scanning have been used in diagnosis, but they all have their limitations; X-rays are also disappointing.
- A qualified manipulator will advise on the need for further investigation where this is necessary.
- Beware of unqualified practitioners.

The normal tail has strength and tone; the horse controls it, and this is reflected in spontaneous movements, such as swishing. A normal tail is not usually held to one side when the horse is moving forwards, nor is it held high, generally, as when the muscles underneath are made dysfunctional by nicking, now illegal in many international jurisdictions.

The tail is an essential indicator of soundness in the nervous system, and when there is evident deviation from a horse's normal strength and movement, then a wider examination is needed to find the cause, and to establish the significance of this to the overall soundness of the horse for a competitive career, and especially for jumping. Many horses with a bent tail, or that hold their tail to one side, perform soundly – although in some, the reaction is an indication of pain as well as of deeper injuries that may require treatment.

10 MUSCLES AND THEIR CARE

Although muscles and bones are dealt with separately for the purposes of this book to help understanding, they are in fact wholly interdependent in the way they work. Also the muscular system of today's horse must put up with more vigorous training regimes that often cause it considerable hardship, the degree of which we often fail to recognise: this intensity does not actually cause lameness, and often only alters the length of stride, its flight pattern, and foot placement – but tendon injuries and lower limb joint and ligament strains are often a direct result of these changes. (To understand the reasons why, see Chapters 2, 8 and 9.)

While the principle problem in this fall is the concrete, muscular injury is likely both from the type of corrective movement, and from getting up afterwards

What Happens in Muscular Injury

An injured muscle swells, and is initially painful to touch and move: the pain is due to exposed pain receptors in the damaged area, and the swelling to the exudation of blood and serum. If the muscle is forced to contract (using electro-stimulation), the pain reaction may be acute.

The horse avoids movement of the injured muscle, and as a consequence, others are recruited to take over its purpose. This alters the stride and puts an uneven and added loading on the compensating muscles. Thus a limb that normally moves in a straight line from footfall to footfall may swing outwardly or inwardly as it goes forwards; the hoof may land at an uneven angle with the ground, and is most likely to land short of its correct position. This can lead to injuries of joints, ligaments and tendons, especially when moving quickly, or jumping.

The effect may be transferred to another limb, most often the diagonal (near hind/off fore) or fellow (near hind/off hind), and the compensating limb may become over-worked by trying to take up the lost power; it may then transfer part of its burden to yet another (usually now a diagonal) limb.

In chronic cases, it is not uncommon to find muscle areas in all four limbs affected by this process.

How Muscular Lameness Happens

The most common direct cause is **unbalanced movement** due to slipping, jumping, falling, or trying to correct errors when they are made at speed – even when a horse is being playful. In such circumstances an **abnormal load** is placed on one or more muscles, and fibres tear.

The extent of the injury depends on the effort involved and, to some extent, the type of muscle and its physical state at the time. Many tears appear to start as minor events involving small groups of fibres in individual muscles, but the **situation is progressive**, and pain in affected sites causes loading on other muscles, which may then incur the same problem. **Fitness matters**, and it is probable that most injuries occur in the earlier stages of a work programme or training (though inevitably some also happen at other times, as in competition).

Muscle injury may also be caused by **too much, or too strenuous, work**, and it often results from **excessive use of particular muscle groups**, for instance the shoulders of horses expected to work on steep inclines, or the muscles on one side of horses that are made to work in one direction only, typically on round gallops.

Injury may also be caused from **working on unsure surfaces**, or **being ridden in shoes that compromise grip**, such as eggbars, heartbars, and wide-webbed shoes without effective grooving. Yet another vulnerable time is when the horse is **going down or getting up after anaesthesia**.

As well as the bent spine, the muscles commonly suffer when a horse falls like this

How the Problem Progresses

Under normal circumstances, an uninjured fore limb is picked up by its flexor muscles (say at the walk), moved forwards by its extensors, and placed a stride length on from its previous position. Without pain or lameness, this is a completely natural reflex process, and the horse does it automatically, without thinking.

The exact spot the foot will land, and its angulation with the ground, is decided by natural stride length as well as other anatomical features, such as conformation. The whole process operates through the reflex arcs, as described in Chapter 8. Any horse has the ability to shorten or lengthen at will. This is calculated from messages going to the brain, and the need is based on everyday matters, such as the avoidance of danger. An involuntary shortening, on the other hand, usually occurs as a result of injury, mostly due to, or in an effort to prevent, pain. This is a protective mechanism intended to prevent further damage to the injured area.

The immediate influence of injury is localised swelling and pain, which may or may not be obvious to the inexperienced eye. The horse alters its stride to avoid using the injured muscle, and recruits others to allow continued forward movement. This may lead to detectable alterations in gait, such as shortening, abduction or adduction (away from, or towards, a straight line) as the limb moves forwards. Nodding lameness is only likely when pain is acute, or when the condition is very advanced. In new cases, when there is obvious lameness, this passes off within a matter of days. However, full muscle repair will not usually occur without treatment, and then the adjustments in gait may be so marginal as to seem insignificant to most people.

The Influence of Pace

As the horse progresses from walk to trot, the workload increases, and a greater recruitment of upper limb muscles comes in as a natural response to calls for increased strength. In trot, the weight of the body has to be lifted higher, and the speed of propulsion demands more power. In the unfit and sedentary state, these upper limb muscles are

When the muscles are well developed by gradual training, tearing is less likely

little used, and hence tend to be undeveloped and slack at the start of a work programme: at this time (in the unfit horse) their fibres are easily torn by excessive or unco-ordinated effort, such as when there is a sudden explosive forward movement, or when the horse slips and has to correct itself.

Workload and Incidence

As the workload for horses that must do fastwork continues to increase – the horse tackling perhaps rising gradients, and jump schooling, and the pace increasing to canter and gallop – the tensions on two main areas become particularly important, namely the shoulders (both behind and in front of the shoulder joint) and the quarters (especially on the roof of the pelvis where the quarter muscles join with the main muscles of the back): these are the areas most commonly, and increasingly, involved in muscular injuries now.

The quarters, as we have already indicated, comprise a pivotal area where tremendous tensions are applied in jumping and galloping; so much so that virtually every horse undergoing intensive training now is at risk of injury. This is not the same as saying that *all* will be injured, or that the incidence of injury has to be as high as it is in horses with manipulable back problems. However, the lack of appreciation of what is happening is certainly influencing incidence, and in some situations – due mostly to unconsidered factors such as gallop design, stiffness, or because of faulty surfaces – the number of injured horses can be significantly high.

Unfortunately, some horses manage to cope despite serious injury, suffering their discomfort while still winning races and competitions. Usually, however, any objective assessment will show a deterioration in

SUMMARY OF PROBABLE CAUSES OF INCREASED MUSCULAR INJURY

- Too much work too soon; cantering before muscles are adequately strong.

- Over-training, maybe too much pace, or too many intervals, and not enough recovery time.

- Also demanding too much from horses; maybe too many competitions.

- All-weather surfaces that lack grip.

- Working on over-steep inclines, and also too fast.

- Diets that may affect muscle metabolism and increase fibre fragility, perhaps due to high protein levels, fat deposition or mineral imbalances.

- Not warming up properly, especially in cold weather.

- The risks increase with speed; also with schooling inadequately prepared horses; and by not understanding the need for muscles to recover from work.

- The fact that strapping is not practised as a regular routine: strapping was the traditional way to treat muscles after work, clearing them of accumulated waste and making them supple again; remember that human athletes need regular massage as an aid to staying sound while they are in intensive muscle training, and the athletic horse is no different in this.

KNOWING YOUR HORSE

For the individual rider, it is important to get to know the natural movement of your horse so as to recognise change from an early stage, then to institute treatment and adjust exercise in a way that helps bring the injured muscle back into full use. The reality is, that any horse in an ascending level of work faces muscle injury as a daily possibility. Awareness is what is needed, because the alternative is a regularly interrupted training programme, constant failure to get to planned competitions, and chronic lameness that may puzzle your vet and perhaps even result in the horse being written off. It may sound exaggerated, but it happens all too often nowadays.

form. Many trainers – significantly of racehorses, but also of show jumpers and dressage horses – constantly bemoan the fact that animals are more prone to injury, and that their competitive life is shortened because of problems with keeping them sound. Indeed, many of these horses come to an end of their career without the real underlying cause being recognised. Moreover treatment is slow, likely to be costly, and will disrupt a training programme.

All this makes the prospect of treatment unpopular, especially as treated horses will re-injure if not regularly monitored, and if the underlying cause (such as a faulty gallops) is not avoided. Many disciplines – for instance eventing, endurance riding, and racing in particular – are driven by economics, and are not yet ready to face the depths of this problem.

Types of Muscle

Cardiac and **smooth** muscle (as in the bowel); neither of these are of direct interest to us in this chapter. **Skeletal** muscle, used in everyday locomotion; it consists of groups of fibres that form muscle bodies, with mixed functions and mixed fibre types – and because of this, a varying exposure to injury.

Types of Skeletal Muscle Fibre

Muscle is composed of three different fibre types, and all three may be found in the same muscle body:
- slow-twitch red fibres that are relatively fatigue-resistant;
- fast-twitch white fibres that fatigue quickly; and
- fast-twitch white fibres that are more resistant to fatigue.

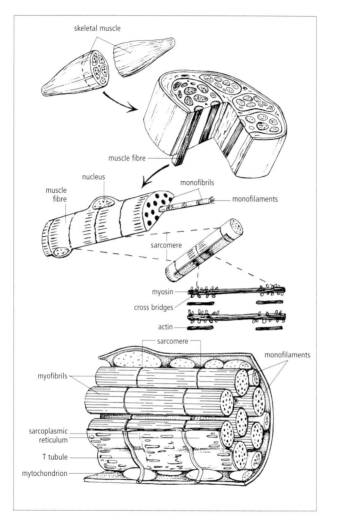

skeletal muscle

muscle fibre

nucleus

muscle fibre

monofibrils

monofilaments

sarcomere

myosin

cross bridges

actin

sarcomere

monofilaments

myofibrils

sarcoplasmic reticulum

T tubule

mytochondrion

Anatomy of skeletal muscle

Generally, fast-twitch fibres are used for speed, and slow-twitch for endurance. However, the different fibre types are frequently mixed in the same muscle body, and this anomaly is further complicated in that skeletal muscles do not usually act in unison, but in groups. What this means is that flexion of a leg, for example, is carried out by a group of flexor muscles at the back of the leg, all taking a share in the workload involved. So if an injury occurs in individual muscles, usually when something untoward happens, this can result in a sudden loss of use of the whole leg (this also happens when a tendon is seriously injured).

In the sedentary, grazing animal, the muscles in use while it ambles about are virtually all slow twitch, and fast-twitch fibres are then progressively conscripted as physical effort increases and the horse trots, canters and gallops. One of the important consequences of getting a horse fit for whatever discipline it is being used for, is the conscription and education of these fibres to react more quickly and to develop more power, and to build reserves of energy in the horse for sustained effort in its work.

Identifying Muscle Groups

Dividing muscles into groups is a purely arbitrary exercise, but such divisions are an essential guide in knowing where to look for the true site of any injury, as we shall see. For the purposes of this exercise we shall put them into three groups: (a), (b) and (c) shown in the diagram.

Though groups (a) and (b) are found to be less prone to injury,

(a) The muscles of the forearms and gaskin: these are always in use as the horse browses and eats; they are innately strong and resistant to injury; some are part of the system that helps the horse to stand while sleeping.

(b) Supporting muscles that play an intermediary role between (a) and (c); some, such as the trapezius and the latissimus dorsi (in the neck and over the ribcage, respectively) are constantly in use, though they are not as often injured as the muscles in (c).

(c) Bulky muscle groups in the quarters (gluteals, for example), neck (brachiocephalicus), and shoulder (triceps): these bear the burden of physically lifting the horse off the ground and propelling it forwards; they are used in fast or heavy work.

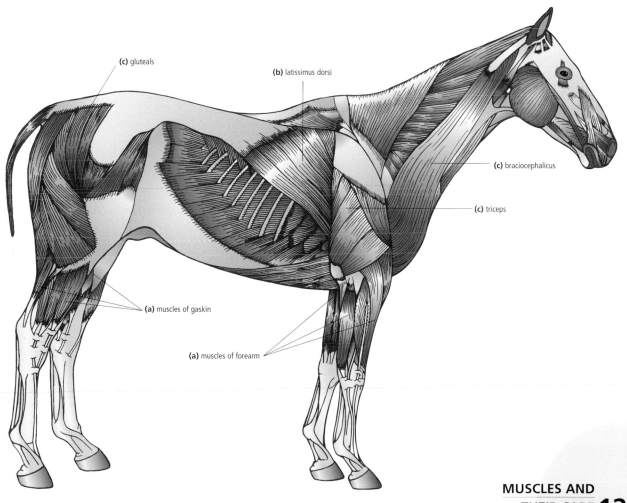

(c) gluteals

(b) latissimus dorsi

(c) braciocephalicus

(c) triceps

(a) muscles of gaskin

(a) muscles of forearm

As the horse moves forward in pace more muscle groups are recruited in order to provide the power

muscle fibres can tear anywhere. Group (c) is most at risk because of muscle size and purpose, and because of losing tone, strength and fitness when a horse is laid off.

As we have said, divisions made on this basis are, of course, purely arbitrary, and the critical differences are in the natural use of each grouping, the types of fibre they contain, and the degrees of strain they are placed under. However, such divisions are an essential guide in knowing where to look for trouble. Most injuries, by the time they are noticed, are of long standing, and it is vital to find the initial, triggering injury, even though this might be in an area quite remote from the more evident, though nonetheless secondary, area as frequently happens. If this isn't done, there may be temporary relief through treatment of the secondary injury, but the horse will go wrong again repeatedly until the original, long-standing injury is identified and treated. The pattern of most common injuries is more easily understood if we consider the daily use of each muscle, those that are least needed in the sedentary or resting state, and how all this changes when a horse is intensively trained.

Progression of Use

At the walk, the horse is using mostly slow-twitch muscle units that are toughened by constant use and by their own physical nature (the forearms, gaskins; also supporting muscles in the neck and back have an anti-gravity function that is ongoing as long as the horse is standing).

At the trot, the effort involves more fast-twitch units, although the number and strength of these will increase with training, making movement easier and more positive as exercise and feeding do their work.

The recruitment of muscles such as the *gluteals* in the quarters (87 per cent fast twitch) increases with pace and effort. Training such muscles to develop is a gradual process that requires patience, as there are no short-cuts. Always follow the principle that a horse should be able to trot strongly before being asked to canter; to canter strongly before being asked to gallop; and to have strengthened its back and quarters before being asked to jump.

Swimming and treadmills are therapies probably only available to larger, professional training establishments; though it is perhaps worthy of note that, while swimming is relatively harmless in healthy, injury-free horses, those with muscular injuries often find the exercise very painful, and it can increase the damage to injured areas.

Lungeing at the trot on a surface that offers good grip is a useful adjunct to therapy in horses with muscular injuries.

Methods of Treatment

A newly injured muscle requires **physical massage**, although the anatomical realities mean that manual massage in horses has a very limited capability. Deep treatment with **lasers** and **ultrasound** penetrates where fingers can't, and their use in chronic lesions is essential to break down adhesions and stimulate a return to working

RECOGNISING MUSCULAR INJURY

- Know the normal anatomy and movement of your horse, and note any changes as soon as they happen.
- Do not ignore sudden loss of action; get used to strapping; look for tender areas, and familiarise yourself with the tone of all muscles.
- Always inspect the muscles after a fall, a slip, or any violent correction.
- Treat any painful areas as suspect, and get expert advice when in doubt.
- Injured areas can be most easily located using electrical stimulation, as with a faradic machine.
- Acute injuries can be detected by various types of scanner, though it may be an expensive way to find a simple answer; also they tend to miss chronic injuries, and do not provide a good overall indication of muscle status.

CASE STUDY A racehorse trainer had a stiff all-weather gallop that started with a right-handed bend. This meant the horses led into it on an off-fore/near-hind diagonal virtually always. There was also a lip on the middle of the steepest part of the incline which demanded an extra effort. From about forty horses, more than half had lameness problems emanating from the near-hind quarter. By the time they were being treated, complications existed in the other hind leg as well as the diagonal forelimb of most.

use. However, this has to be combined with some form of **stimulation** to force the injured muscle back into use – it is the depth of the lesions that is critical, and the injuries will recur if not fully dispersed and cured. Unfortunately, many **modern electrical machines** (such as interferential, **h-wave** and **faradism**) tend only to stimulate surface tissues, and do not get deep enough into injured areas; the results are therefore often disappointing.

In a new injury, it is important to be aware that it may be **chronic areas remote from the injured site** that have caused it, and inevitably this is likely to affect the success of treatment. Horses with advanced injuries are likely to suffer chronic pain; this becomes evident when successful treatment brings them back to pain-free normality. However, be advised that many chronic quarter lesions have a tendency to become calcified, thus making treatment more protracted. A first-time injury, recently incurred, may come out relatively easily with rest, massage and gentle exercise; but **the horse may be left with an altered gait** that will only lead to further trouble.

Physical treatment must therefore be accompanied by a **programme of exercise** that completes the **rehabilitation of the injured muscle**; thus the horse must do no more than he is capable of, for the stage of his recovery – for instance he should only trot until limb movement has

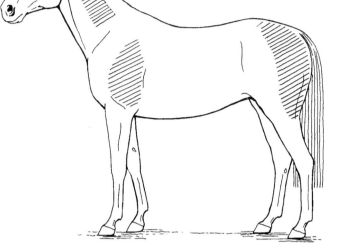

Strapping is an essential means of preventing muscle injuries. The shading on the illustrations indicates the muscle areas on which you should concentrate

PREVENTION OF MUSCLE INJURIES

- Strap your horse for fifteen minutes each limb on a daily basis, but especially after strenuous exercise, competitions or jumping.

- Use a qualified physiotherapist when there is an injury, and always have the muscles checked when you suspect injury, or are in doubt.

- Always warm up properly before work; a good brisk trot is the most natural way of doing this.

- There should always be a gentle warm-down, such as an active ten-minute walk, to help the body get rid of waste products that stiffen muscles after work.

- Feed sensibly, use electrolytes regularly and judiciously, and avoid complicated feeds and excessively high protein levels.

- After any enforced break, return to full work gradually, providing at least a week of build-up for each week of lay-off.

returned fully to normal, as cantering too soon only frustrates this aim. Also horses coming out of pain with treatment can become very playful, and put on weight quickly, and they need special care and attention to reduce the risk of new injuries just from over-exuberance; so therefore always exercise in protective boots.

In short, restart a work programme gradually; do not progress too quickly; allow the horse to redevelop his strength steadily; and finally, do not jump or gallop until he is ready for it.

Tying Up, or Azoturia

Tying up usually occurs as a clinical crisis that needs immediate attention from your vet. There are degrees of suffering, and in the worst instance a horse may have to be boxed home, or even left where he is.

Signs

The principle symptom of tying up is progressive stiffening. This may cause a horse to pull up while working, or it may occur after he has stopped, or even after returning home. The extent of this varies, and severe cases may be unable to move and will be very distressed.

What to Do

- Immediately a horse ties up, cover him with a rug and keep him warm.
- If he can walk, take him back quietly to his stable, and call your vet.
- If he is in acute pain after work, do not walk him, but call a vet quickly and arrange to transport him home, if he can be loaded.
- The vet will relieve the pain, and try to ease the immediate crisis.
- Immediately cut back on solid feed; provide just a small warm mash and hay.
- If possible, walk him out the next day for a bite of grass, but consult your vet if in doubt. Long term stabling is often the wrong advice.
- His return to work will be based on his response, on the cause of his tying up, and if this can be easily corrected.
- Critically assess his diet, and as work is resumed, feed only simple concentrates that are low in protein and oil, and meadow hay.
- Dispersing the muscle lesions with strapping and physiotherapy will help this condition.

CAUSES OF AZOTURIA

- The earliest cases were reported in working horses that were stabled at weekends and kept on full rations; when returned to work, they went stiff (this was commonly known as Monday morning disease). The problem was therefore nutritional: too much food when there was no exercise.
- The condition today has changed face, which is not surprising, and the causes, whilst still basically nutritional, are more complex, and can be due to particular types of feed or ways of feeding (too much protein or oil, for example); also because of deficiencies of calcium; or after liver disease; or because, possibly, of toxins coming from water.
- Many cases are misdiagnosed, and confusion exists between ordinary muscle tears and tying up, when opinions rely too heavily on blood results.

11 LAMENESS and routine prevention

The differences between draught work on cobbled streets and riding on country lanes are self–evident

Many people believe that the majority of lamenesses in the horse arise from problems in the feet, most commonly the fore feet, or between the knee and the ground in front, or the hock and the ground behind. These ideas, often supported by statistics, are accumulated from sources where, it has to be suspected, there is no allowance made for muscular and spinal lamenesses as considered here.

Horses Past and Present

The origins of this perception came from a time when knowledge was more primitive, and there was a huge population of working horses, many drawing cabs and drays on cobbled streets, and whose lamenesses were indeed likely to have been associated with the foot. We think of conditions such as navicular disease that, if it ever was a cause of lameness, could easily have been related to pounding on surfaces that were hard, often undulating, and which offered little grip. But vets in the old days were as divided as they are today on the significance of this condition, your writer being a confirmed sceptic.

Few, if any, horses today have to undergo that type of trauma. Ours are ridden on levelled surfaces, such as cambered tarmac; we give great consideration to foot wear, and there is a general understanding that concussion has to be limited, feet kept well balanced, and that horses should not be ridden on hard surfaces except within the strictest of limitations. Today's horse is unlikely ever to experience any surface that compares with the cobblestones of the last century, nor to have to work eight hours at a stretch coping with them. His life is very different from a vanner that had to earn his keep perhaps six days a week, pulling and pounding, with no allowance possible for the threat posed underfoot. Just think of the effect of walking on a hard surface that constantly bends your ankles.

Today's horse, by comparison, is an athlete that runs, jumps, races and competes on varied prepared surfaces, performing different acts of physical exercise, and using, in the main, different and more highly developed muscle groups in order to satisfy our demands. It is not logical that the sources of his lameness should be the same as a vanner's. Only the hunter and racehorse were comparable athletes a hundred years ago, even if the family pony was fit and active when drawing the trap, and the working horse had to be kept strong in order to pull a plough. Perhaps, if the criterion is nodding lameness, the foot might be a common source, but changes of stride and pain in movement have to be seen as of equal importance if the horse is to go forwards freely and be able to compete and perform to the ability he possesses.

Evaluating Lameness

There is a need to anticipate lameness every time a horse is taken out of its box. Any change from normal action may indicate lameness, and has to be recognised and evaluated quickly. A rider is often the best judge, and the information he or she may provide should form the basis of any history-taking.

The distinction between nodding lameness, where pain comes as a foot touches the ground, and what is sometimes called 'swinging leg' lameness, where pain comes as the limb moves forwards, is critical to the whole discovery of the source. It is only once the limb has been identified that an examination can progress to finding the specific area.

Where the immediate source is not evident, the horse should be stood square on a level surface for inspection. Any indication that he favours a leg could be significant, though it may not; persistent resting of one leg is a strong indicator, as is reluctance to bear weight (when picking out the feet, the horse may resist lifting a sound leg that makes it transfer added weight onto a lame one).

Pointing a toe can mean pain at the heel, although acute pain at the toe may have the same effect; thus this stance only means there is pain that may be eased by taking up this particular position.

Nodding Lameness

With a fore limb, the head is raised as the affected limb takes weight at the walk or trot; it drops as weight is transferred to a sound limb.

With a hind limb, the hip on the affected side rises, and this too returns to normal when weight is transferred onwards.

This is typical of foot lameness, but also of injured bones, joints or ligaments – in short, when there is any acute sensation of pain brought on by weight-bearing, or any movement that risks increased trauma to injured tissues: the horse protects the injured part by limiting the weight load and preventing further injury. For instance at the walk, when the

QUESTIONS TO ASK WHEN ASSESSING LAMENESS

- Is lameness evident while the horse is at rest?
- If not, does it show at the walk or trot?
- Is lameness accompanied by head nodding when weight is borne?
- If not, is the stride shortened, or does the leg swing unusually in movement?
- Could there be more than one limb involved?
- Are the symptoms permanent or intermittent?
- Is the lameness more marked on hard or soft surfaces?
- Is it more marked on rising or falling ground?
- Is lameness increased when the horse is ridden?
- Is lameness more prominent on one or other diagonal?
- Does the horse come out of the stable lame, or only become lame as it progresses?
- Does the lameness go as the horse warms up?
- Does the horse resent putting weight on a leg when it is at rest?
- Is there any history of a fall or some other mishap, such as a slip or a kick?
- When was the horse last shod?

(*right*) As a lame forelimb takes the horse's weight his head will rise

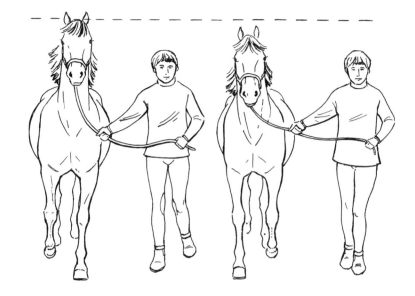

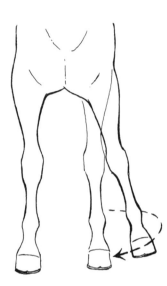

Note the flight path of the foot as the horse moves

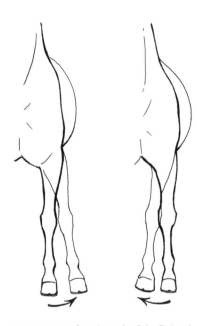

Rotation outwards or inwards of the flight of the foot may indicate shoulder lameness

lame limb bears weight, the horse will try to avoid putting weight on a toe or heel that is painful.

To assess lameness, look separately from in front, from behind and from the side, especially in more subtle lamenesses. Only gauge the movement of the head when the horse approaches, as the head drops when a lame hind limb takes weight, and the timing and nature of the way it lifts is critical in deciding which is significant. There is no need to trot a horse with evident lameness; it may only make matters worse.

Swinging Leg Lameness

Upper limb lamenesses are typified by an altered flight pattern in the paces. First, look at the horse standing and note its balance, whether there is any sign of discomfort, and if there are variations in its surface anatomy caused by wasted areas or swellings.

Then have the horse walked away and back for about 20 to 30m: observe the flight of each limb, rather than the reaction when weight is borne, which may be misleading; changes from the known, natural action are critical. **Shoulder lameness** may be marked by rotation outwards or inwards; the tracking, as seen from a side view, is likely to be short; there may even be detectable nodding as the stride lengthens.

If **the neck** is injured, its mobility and the horse's balance may be impaired: this may be evident when riding, or when the horse tries a simple procedure such as scratching itself; all such signs are likely to have a bearing. Unfortunately, anatomical changes to the shoulder and neck may not be easy to detect, as direct comparison of the areas isn't that easy.

Upper hind limb lameness may be marked by physical effort as the leg engages and before it is lifted from the ground; tracking may again be short when seen from the side. Also, upper hind limb lamenesses are marked by swellings and wasting that are evident at pelvic level.

When **both fore limbs** are lame, there is a shuffling gait and the head is unable to respond as before; the same thing can happen in the hind limbs.

Examining a Limb

In many cases the source of lameness is apparent and easily detected. The lame limb may be immediately obvious, and there may be swelling on a joint or a tendon that is an evident indicator. However, it isn't uncommon to find passive filling in lower limb areas that may indicate nothing more than venous stasis (the blood not returning up the limb), and so it becomes important to read beyond the immediate signs.

Having located the suspect limb (or limbs), examine it in detail for **swellings, heat, pain or wasting,** starting at the foot and working upwards. To be significant, filling over a joint will be warm, there will be pain on passive movement, and nodding lameness at the walk or trot. **Tendon injuries** are associated with pain on finger pressure, though there may not be nodding lameness in either slight or settled cases.

Manually examine the whole limb, feeling each joint individually, looking for reactions from the horse, but being objective – some will anticipate pain and pull the limb away even when nothing is wrong.

■ EVALUATING HEAT, SWELLING AND PAIN

Pain and heat are both good indicators of the seriousness of an injury. Critical detection of heat is an acquired talent, but when a lower limb injury is acute, there will also be pain on finger pressure, and the horse will be clearly lame at the walk.

Passive filling in a lower limb could result from a **graze or a wound** further up the leg; it can also occur from **digestive problems**, or **lymphangitis**, both of which are unrelated, the difference being that usually more than one limb will be filled in dietary cases; moreover lymphangitis is often complex, and will need your vet to help sort it out.

An **active filling associated with a new injury** is always tender to the touch in the critical area; it may be linked to passive filling further up; or fluid may drain downwards, sometimes creating the impression of spreading infection. Always consider the **possibility of infection** once the skin has been penetrated and there is a painful swelling; what may seem like an acute new injury might in fact be the result of a thorn prick at an earlier time. Pain in movement expresses itself differently from pain when bearing weight, and is more difficult to detect.

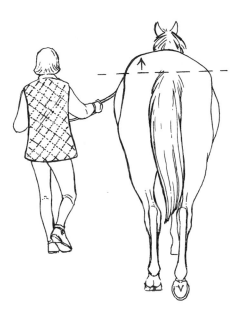

Signs of physical effort in lifting a back leg, and sometimes swelling, indicate upper hind limb lameness

Swelling of the lower limbs may indicate a wound further up the leg

Lameness in the Foot

In any acute foot condition the horse feels pain when the foot bears weight, and will snatch it up in any kind of movement: the impression of pain is easy to see, and this may be evident as the horse moves over in the stable, when it turns, or at any time it should bear weight. A similar reaction may occur when a shoe has moved and the sole is taking direct pressure, or there is a corn; it will also occur in conditions such as ringbone, or in joint injuries.

With most foot conditions there will be heat to the touch, either generally over the foot, or localised over one particular part, such as a nail track, or a heel, or at any point where there has been a puncture wound. Note that there can be as much heat from a bruise or a bone fracture as from an infection.

Pain can often be located just by finger pressure on the sole or heel; otherwise a hoof tester may be used in order to apply a higher degree of localised pressure.

Not uncommonly, the affected leg may fill above the foot, perhaps to mid-cannon, particularly in infections; when this happens it often looks as if the injury is in the tendon. The blood vessels running down the back of the cannon on either side will usually be thick and throbbing.

TREATING THE FOOT

Any kind of foot pain is crippling and may require veterinary attention; the following course of action should be pursued:

- If there is a shoe on, have it taken off.
- Ask your farrier or vet to search for a puncture hole or infection source.
- If nothing is found, the vet may take X-rays, or carry out other tests.
- If pus appears, poultice the foot and leave the shoe off until the infection has cleared and the foot has cooled down; renew the poultice every twelve hours.
- If there is no pus, and the foot is still warm, poultice anyway, in case the infection is only developing and pus has not yet accumulated – as will happen after a puncture wound or when a horse is pricked while being shod.
- Make sure there is protection against tetanus.
- Your vet will decide if antibiotic therapy is needed.

THRUSH

This is an infection involving the frog, which produces a smelly black exudate and can undermine sensitive tissues and as a result cause chronic lameness.

An important aspect of treatment is to keep the underfoot conditions clean and dry, and to remove rotted frog tissue, opening up pockets that might occlude air and so allow organisms to grow. Depending on its severity, the condition may respond to an antibiotic spray, or solutions of copper sulphate, formalin, iodine or phenol; your vet should advise you.

Thrush is sometimes a problem when horses wear rubber, plastic or leather pads under their shoes for long periods, as the air cannot circulate, and dirt may get trapped between foot and pad.

CASE STUDY

Pedal osteitis is a common cause of foot lameness, mainly in the fore feet, and is a consequence of concussion. It is painful and affected horses usually show a shuffling lameness, especially when it affects both feet. Diagnosis is made by X-ray and there are changes to the bone, which may be demineralised, or there can be spurs seen, usually in the region of the heels.

Such a horse was presented for examination. The feet were shrunken (not contracted) and the horse moved with evident pain. X-rays revealed a demineralised bone.

It was decided to use a low dose of pulsed ultrasound, treating each foot while submersed in water. After a couple of weeks, the feet seemed to expand and there was far greater freedom in movement. This progress was maintained and X-rays taken at a later stage showed significant remineralisation of the bone. The horse was subsequently used as a hack and was never reported lame again.

Identifying Less Obvious Nodding Lameness

Chronic foot pain can come from degenerative conditions such as **pedal osteitis, sidebone,** or **low ringbone,** where there will be persistent heat, even with a lower grade of lameness than in foot infection. Examine each area of the foot and leg in detail, looking for heat, swelling and pain: if the pain is acute and can't be localised, call your vet; if the foot is cold and pain free, feel the coronet, pastern and fetlock using the palm of the hand, noting in particular the **sesamoid area** at the back of the fetlock.

Run your knuckles down the front of the cannon, in order to check for **sore shins**; don't be rough: use a gentle but firm contact. Feel the **tendons** and **suspensory ligament** through their length, first to detect heat; if nothing is found, lift the leg and use gentle finger pressure to detect pain.

Rotate the **fetlock joint** gently, watching the reaction of the horse; he will pull on the leg if there is pain.

Feel along the **splint bones** and press the fingers into any evident hard swelling: a splint is a bony lump where the splint bone meets the cannon, and there is usually a reaction to finger pressure in splint lameness. Also check the **balance of the foot**, especially in mature horses, as there is a positive link between this and the formation of splints.

With the foot back on the ground, feel the front, sides and back of **the knee**, noting any fluid swelling, heat or sensitivity to touch.

Closely inspect the **forearm, elbow** and **shoulder** areas for surface injury, or painful areas, swellings or obvious deformities; nerve damage will lead to paralysis and distortion of the surface anatomy. Place the palm over the elbow and shoulder joints and feel for heat, swelling or pain.

Go through the same procedure in the **hind limb**, concentrating especially on the **hock** and **stifle**; the hip is so deep anatomically that changes may be difficult to detect.

A bony lump where the splint meets the cannon (on the right of the upper part of the bone)

Check swellings to assess whether they are hot and whether they are hard or soft

Tendon Injuries

Tendon injuries occur because tendon fibres are asked to stretch further than their natural capacity allows. Tendon tissue is considerably less elastic than muscle, but stronger and probably less commonly damaged. The traditional perception is that an injured tendon is always weaker after repair, though this does not have to be the case.

All sorts of treatments have been recommended, from physiotherapy

First principles The first principle of treating an injured joint is to provide support and limit movement. Joints such as the fetlock and knee are relatively easy to bandage, but every joint has its own anatomical peculiarities. The idea is to help hold injured tissues in apposition so the body can heal them naturally, although a major problem is the influence of gravity pulling torn tissue ends apart as an area moves; this principally applies to transverse, rather than longitudinal tissue damage.

Cold compresses may be used at the start to limit swelling, and healing is greatly helped by the use of a laser or ultrasound to stimulate repair. The extent of any joint injury may need to be investigated by your vet, using X-rays or other diagnostic tests; the degree of lameness will tell you.

coffin joint in foot	Not easily supported, so may need something like a plaster cast to limit movement.
pastern and fetlock	Depending on degree of injury, may need the same kind of immobilisation, though external support is often enough.
knee	With acute injuries, consider the possibility of fracture; veterinary examination is necessary when there is heat, swelling and evident pain on weight bearing.
elbow and shoulder	Not that frequently sprained – which is just as well, since they cannot be supported as the lower limb joints can, neither can they be immobilised.
hock	A complex joint not dissimilar from the knee, the major difference being function, as the hock is the spring that unleashes a great deal of explosive forward power; supporting the joint is difficult because of its anatomy. Any hock lameness merits advice from your vet.
stifle	Possesses the equivalent of the kneecap, and is a more complicated ligamentous structure than most other joints; locking of the stifle is a recognised occurrence that is sometimes relieved by surgery.
hip joint	Not often sprained, though fractures may occur, in which case the prognosis would be poor; diagnosis will require an X-ray or scan.

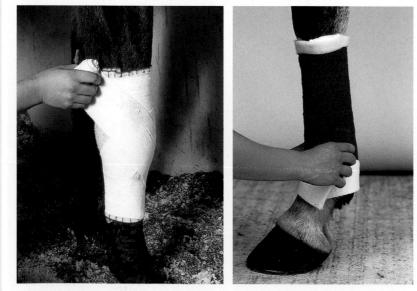

(*far left*) Sprains to the knee are helped by support, although full investigation will be needed

(*left*) Support bandages must be evenly applied and the use of padding will prevent adverse reactions

Tendon injury may result from landings like this

to firing, from injections to surgery, and your long-term choices will be influenced by advice on these. However, a critical consideration is the relationship between the tendon and the leg as a whole. There are good grounds for believing that many tendon injuries arise from lost limb elasticity following muscle problems, and that the best way to prevent recurrence is to treat the muscles and tendons as a unit. When this is done, most tendons do not rupture again.

Causes

Injuries occur for a variety of reasons, the simplest to understand being when a foot drops into a hole while the horse is travelling at speed, and the leg bends further than it is naturally able to. They also happen as a result of trauma, as, for example, when they are struck into from behind.

As mentioned above, tendon injuries often occur as a consequence of muscular injuries. This may also happen when an injured muscle is not the attached muscle, but one whose loss leads to the same end result: it is the loss of elasticity in the limb that creates the problem.

Diagnosis

The immediate signs are self-evident, though they could be confused with localised infection over the same area. Your vet may decide to scan the injury, both for diagnostic reasons and to monitor progress. The procedure is not without its flaws, though good information is always best when there is doubt; but interpretations can differ, and some false pictures can be created.

MAINTAINING JOINTS

In show-jumpers particularly, where the joints are subjected to considerable stress, it has become common practice to routinely monitor signs of degeneration and to use treatments, frequently in the form of injections placed directly into the joint, to stimulate repair and restore normal functional health. This is too complex an issue to discuss here, and any such treatment must only be considered in consultation with your vet. The risk associated with any such procedure is that it becomes a fashion – when only time can decide on its realistic, practical effectiveness. Besides, it is a dubious practice to inject normal joints because of undiagnosed lameness in a limb or limbs.

Hocks are often injected because a horse isn't moving well, although the problem may be in the quarters. Sacro-iliac joints, too, are injected, when the logic for doing so can be seriously disputed. And there is a fashion to ply horses with supplements aimed at improving joint function. If there is no problem, this must be wasteful, as many are finding to their cost.

- Treat the immediate injury with cold hosing and compresses, and apply strong support for the first two days; also support the unaffected leg. Do not over-tighten bandages: avoid this happening by using padding (such as Gamgee) underneath them; make sure you have enough, and that it is evenly distributed.

- From the second day, treat the injury with a laser or ultrasound, staying away from the centre and concentrating on the outer limits of the swelling. The cold treatment may be discontinued, but retain support at all times.

- So far, all you are trying to do is to reduce inflammation, and there is no question of repair yet.

- Cut out concentrates and feed only hay and water; keep the horse stabled, and never without leg support.

- No matter how good the leg looks after a week or two, do not resume riding without clearance from your vet (a laser may mask the symptoms).

- Once the limb is cold and not painful to touch – though a period of at least three to four weeks should be allowed to elapse, even if the healing process is quicker than this – the horse should be walked out to help healing; consult your vet.

- Turn out only when the injury is fully settled and there is no risk of aggravation.

- Treatment of the muscle/tendon unit should begin in the first week, and be continued until repair is completed; this way the heat will dissipate more quickly, and a stronger repair will be achieved; the horse will also be able to be led out, and turned out sooner.

- Horses with collapsed heels or excessively upright conformation might be helped by corrective shoeing.

- A six-month lay-off is considered sensible, though this can be reduced with good physiotherapy.

Suspensory Ligament Injury

As the suspensory ligament is not a tendon and does not have muscular connections, injuries are treated in the same way as any ligament. There is every hope of complete recovery as long as there are no evident anatomical weaknesses, such as low heels or upright limbs.

WHAT TO DO WITH SUSPENSORY LIGAMENT INJURIES

- First, control heat and swelling, and provide support; then use a laser or ultrasound.

- Keep the horse stabled, and feed on hay and water.

- Anatomically, a point of weakness is the attachment to the sesamoid bones, and strong, continued support may be necessary to aid recovery.

- A Patten shoe may need to be applied, depending on severity,

and the horse stood in until repair is complete: this takes about six weeks.

- Allow the horse to stand in for a few more days after the support is removed and the Patten shoe taken off.

- Then just walk for a few more days, and only trot in hand on a firm surface to check for lameness before progressing.

- Return to full work slowly and with care.

Treating Injured Sesamoids

The critical factor in sesamoid injury, after accurate diagnosis, is providing adequate support so that the bone ends are held in contact; repair must also be stimulated. Healing will normally be complete in six weeks, even where there are fractures.

Lameness Prevention

It is clear that lameness goes with the sport, and there can be no way to prevent a horse from slipping or falling in competition or training. However, there are precautions that can be taken and which will help limit the risk. Inevitably a horse that is feeling pain in his back or in his muscles won't jump as well as he might, in the same way as one with unbalanced feet or an ill-fitting shoe is subject to pain. It is attention to detail and the understanding of pain that can make a difference, and horses are telling us this all the time by the way they perform.

Points of Note

- Make sure the feet are properly balanced and shod to meet the conformational needs of the limb; that is, be sure that limb balance is placed before foot balance where there is any conformational problem.

- Use regular strapping to keep the muscles supple, and treat any muscle tears by physiotherapy as they occur.

- Have the back manipulated as required, depending on need, altered action, reluctance and pain.

- Warm up before any serious work with brisk, active paces over an adequate time period.

- Make sure you pace the horse on stiff inclines: he should not be made to go faster than his fitness allows.

- Avoid unstable surfaces that do not provide adequate grip, especially at faster paces.

- Do not swim horses that have muscular or back injuries, nor subject them to exercises they cannot readily handle; learn to recognise upper body pain and abnormal movement, even at the walk, which emanates from the pelvis and shoulders.

- Avoid ground conditions in competition that are likely to cause injury: too hard or too heavy.

WHAT TO DO WITH INJURED SESAMOIDS

- The horse should be stabled and fed just hay and water.

- Have a Patten shoe fitted.

- Support the joint with a strong bandage.

- Treat the immediate symptoms as previously to reduce inflammation and swelling; then use a laser or ultrasound to stimulate repair.

SHOEING TIPS

- Remove or replace shoes too soon, rather than too late. Once a shoe has moved inside its position of support from the walls, the sole is immediately at risk of being brusied or penetrated. If the clenches loosen, the shoe may come off, in which case it could stick into the foot and do untold damage.

- It is a false economy to leave shoes on too long, not only because of the effects of movement, but because unevenly worn shoes may disrupt limb balance and so cause injury to joints and/or ligaments.

Using Physiotherapy

Never use any kind of physiotherapy equipment without proper advice and instruction.

ADVANTAGES AND DISADVANTAGES

All these forms of treatment are used extensively in human physiotherapy and have been transferred empirically to use in the equine field. The clinical success of lasers, ultrasound and faradic stimulation has become increasingly recognised over recent decades, while the usefulness of more modern equipment is dictated by tissue penetration and enduring tissue repair. One of the principal disadvantages of equine physiotherapy is that it is time consuming and labour intensive; a course of treatment for chronically damaged muscles will take anything up to six weeks, with sessions on individual animals taking in the region of an hour, and having to be repeated at least three times weekly.

It also suffers from the fact that to date, there have been no qualifications in animal sports physiotherapy, and knowledge has been largely inadequate in this field. With proper advice, however, there is no reason why any conscientious horse owner cannot use remedial equipment on specific routine conditions common in athletic horses; many yards have their own lasers, ultrasounds, muscle stimulators and also magnetic field equipment.

Physiotherapy is a complementary field to standard scientific medicine; it is used after a diagnosis has been made, and after other specific treatments recommended by your vet, perhaps for pain control and reducing inflammation. Hot and cold applications have a standard part to play in physiotherapy; cold treatment, in the form of ice packs, or cold hosing, may be very effective in reducing the immediate tissue reactions after trauma.

The essence of physiotherapy is treatment that is then followed by rehabilitation: the injured part is repaired, and then returned to full working use; and this involves a routine of gradual and increasing exercises until complete working soundness is resumed.

Local treatment of muscular injuries is only partly effective without exercise; the pain will be relieved, but a full working recovery in the athletic horse will not occur without reversing the effects of injury and restoring natural action. In the same way, an injured joint or tendon has to be gradually returned to use, so that they, too, are not subjected to maximal stresses until strong enough to take them. Thus while being treated, the injured horse will undergo a course of rehabilitative exercises: for instance, he will have to extend himself at the trot for anything up to an hour each day, preferably on the lunge (he should not canter, however).

Immediate return to high intensity work will only risk re-injury.

Equipment in Physiotherapy

The equipment used in physiotherapy is extensive, and in the human field extends to a far wider range than could ever be used on horses. The principal practical applications for equine use are first, **muscle stimulators**, and also **ultrasound** and **lasers** that work on the skin or have a penetrating effect into deeper tissues; these stimulate blood flow, break down adhesions and organise repair.

Interferential and **high frequency currents** are used for their ability to stimulate circulation and aid local repair, mostly in muscle injuries, although they also have an affect in other situations; their weakness would appear to be in their depth of penetration in the kind of muscle injuries common in horses.

Magnetic field therapy is also used in much the same situations, and with the same drawbacks: it suffers from the fact that muscle is not stimulated, therefore it only reduces inflammation and pain, but does not bring muscle back into use.

■ LASERS AND ULTRASOUND

Lasers are now used as a routine preventive on legs after competition, although the practice might be more in hope than good sense: if there is damaged tissue, the symptoms may be hidden and the horse returned to work too quickly, thus risking even more serious consequences.

■ Ultrasonic machines should always be used with the utmost care and responsibility: they can be dangerous in the wrong hands, and can cause irreparable tissue damage if improperly used. The following points should be observed:

■ Never use an ultrasound for at least twenty-four hours after the injury is sustained, then use only on a pulsed mode, and keep the frequency as low as is compatible with repair.

■ Keep the treatment head away from the centre of injury for the first few days, gradually bringing it closer, day by day.

■ Ultrasound use on fresh tendon injuries can cause acute pain over the torn area.

■ Faulty techniques can cause catastrophic damage to both soft tissues and bone.

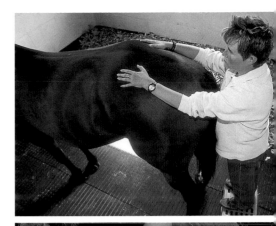

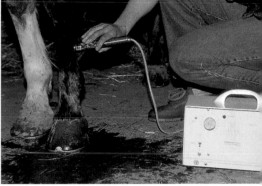

■ CONDITIONS SUITABLE FOR ULTRASOUND OR LASER TREATMENT:

■ Any kind of skin wound, especially slow-healing types; but do not use an ultrasound over an infected site.

■ Joint and/or ligament injuries; also provide good support, and rest the horse until the condition is fully repaired.

■ Sesamoiditis, though as part of a full reparatory process: thus provide support, rest the horse, and also take the pressure off the part with a raised shoe.

■ Any non-infectious swelling on any part of the body other than the eye and the spine.

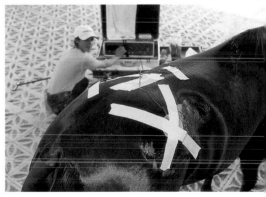

(*from top*) All types of therapy have their use in treating injuries: manual; ultrasound and faradic

■ CONTRAINDICATIONS

■ Do not use ultrasound on infections or haematomas of recent origin (a clot may be disturbed and cause fresh bleeding).

■ Be careful when using ultrasound over bone; always act on the basis of detailed and qualified advice regarding frequencies, modes and treatment times.

■ Both lasers and ultrasound will ease pain and also effectively reduce inflammation; however, lasers can reduce heat and swelling perhaps too quickly from an injury, so encouraging the belief that repair is complete, and perhaps leading to a too-early return to work, and so renewed injury.

12 DAILY HEALTH MANAGEMENT

The horse is an animal of apparently opposing requirements: it thrives on a dependable routine in the yard and stable, but is easily bored by repetitive exercises; indeed, many derive their greatest pleasure from the varied action and changing terrains of a day's hunting. Note that routine is not the same as boredom, and boredom in the stable – if he is not taken out enough, or allowed out in the field, or if his stable has no outlook, or if he is left on his own hour after hour – can lead to the development of vices; in a similar way, monotonous exercises over the same ground can cause those with a reluctant streak to lay down tools and refuse to be trained.

So there are two sides to the need for routine: the horse has his inner clock set for his owner's arrival in the yard and the first feed of the day, but his love of routine fades if it means walking the same roads, galloping the same fields and spending hours in the same school or walker. Thus routines are best kept for the stable, and variety for work and play.

Many derive great pleasure from the varied action and changing terrains of a day's hunting

Stabling

The importance of proper stabling and also a suitable environment increases with the intensity of work and the type of physical demands being made. So a stabled broodmare with a woolly coat needs less warmth indoors, and might well thrive better outdoors in reasonable weather conditions. On the other hand, a clipped horse hard trained for racing or eventing can be very susceptible to cold, and will use a significant amount of consumed food simply for the maintenance of body heat if his stable is cold and drafty. Transfer the same horse to a warmer stable, still on the same rations, and he might put on condition, maybe even get too hot to the point of sweating if dressed in the same rugs and blankets. But transfer him from a warm to a cold stable, and he may quickly lose weight – and almost inevitably he will show signs of infection before very long.

The Ideal Stable for the Athletic Horse

The most comfortable stables have **insulated walls, ceiling and floor**, and **the vents are not fixed** so they can be closed or adjusted. There will be no damp patches due to faulty interior finishes, porous surfaces or blocked rain chutes. Inside, the stable will be fully separated from other stables, and have no communicating vents or grills, or any other means of creating cross-flows of air.

One exception to this ideal might be where two stables are treated as a single unit, with each end wall sealed, and the unit treated as one entity for the sake of environment control. Back wall vents (opposite the door) will only be used when the weather dictates, and sparingly, if ever, in winter.

Windows will be used to meet external conditions and adjusted as needed. Air entry will ideally come from the front only, and will exit by a small ceiling vent into a roof space or loft (never directly to the outside).

The **floor** will be free-draining so that urine can escape.

Half doors are generally preferable to whole doors, but the tops will be used like windows, adjusted according to weather requirements, and perhaps only fully closed in the very extremes of winter (though even then the need for air exchange must be observed, to ensure the stable doesn't become too stuffy during the course, say, of a long night).

Old-style wooden boxes can be warm, and will provide heat and weather protection. **Modern wooden boxes**, on the other hand, are frequently uninsulated and usually draughty, besides which many are over-ventilated, with fixed vents that cannot be adjusted.

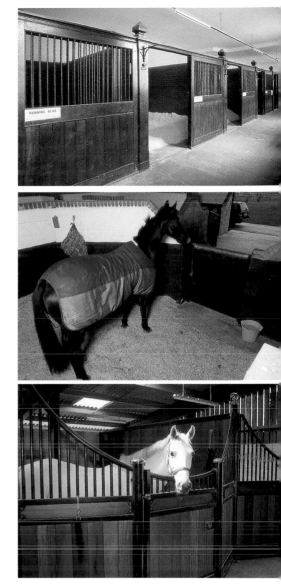

The maintenance of a reasonable temperature versus the need for ventilation is a chief concern when choosing stabling. These three examples may be warm and airy, but there is a danger of infection running rife in conditions where single stables cannot be isolated

HOW TO IMPROVE BARN STABLING

- The environment within a barn inevitably varies according to climate and the prevailing weather conditions. In warm and humid countries, there may be a regular need for extensive ventilation, even at night. But in colder climes there is invariably a night-time chill factor, even in summer, and winter is marked by extreme changes of temperature, windflows, dampness and so on, on an hour-to-hour basis. The purpose of a stable is to provide environmental stability in all these things, and to protect the horse from wide variations that his body has trouble adjusting to.

- A human body takes between six and ten hours to adjust to a temperature change of 5 degrees, a process that it is believed may directly inhibit the immune system; and there is no reason to suspect the horse is any different in this. Trained horses, particularly, are at risk because of what we demand of them – and not forgetting the fact that many of them spend more than 90 per cent of their lives confined in a space where they can't even move about to keep themselves warm without being said to have a vice.

- The typical French-American-style barn has a lofted space over the horses, which has the effect of reducing airflows, and each stall is a completely separate unit, with the exception of a common airspace that they look into in the aisles. On the basis of anecdotal evidence, this seems to be a most effective system, reducing the incidence of respiratory disease, presumably by reducing airflows around the horse and allowing greater warmth.

Barns

Inevitably, most of the requirements listed under the previous heading cannot be met in open or partly closed barns with fixed, open vents and no means of controlling airflows. Yet barns are here to stay: they are cheaper to build, allow greater comfort for stable staff to work in, and the horses are all able to see each other. There are, however, clear disadvantages from the horse's viewpoint:

- Since there is no environment control, if the building is cold, this will affect all the horses.
- With fixed open vents, heat cannot be retained within the building.
- Should any horse fall sick, there are no barriers to the spread of infection.
- An allergic horse cannot be kept free of allergens, unless all the others are subjected to the same precautions.

Bedding

Fashions are constantly changing as far as bedding is concerned, dictated by ease of use, disposability, freedom from dust, and the comfort provided for the horse. However, ammonia in urine is a respiratory irritant, and faeces carry organisms, worm eggs and larvae, so hygiene is critical; moreover it is important that, whatever the type of bedding, its influence on the immediate environment is beneficial.

Important Points

- Ideally, a **stable floor** should be insulated and free draining, and should not retain the horse's excreta.
- **Bedding should provide a warm surface** that the horse can lie on without injuring himself; it should be easy to maintain, and pose no health hazards for either the horse or his keeper.
- **Rubberised floors** are increasingly used as a basis on which to lay a bed; problems arise, however, if the rubber isn't sealed down and excreta get underneath.
- **Straw** has always been the traditional bedding, providing a warm and protective shield to lie on – although its quality is subject to the weather at harvest time, and to the conditions in which it is stored. Its inherent disadvantages are that it may trigger disease, and also the horse's tendency to eat it (which may be prevented by applying disinfectant to the surface).
- **Deep-litter systems** have a tendency to cause dampness and create smells; not the best option for competition horses or racehorses.

■ Any form of bedding must be judged according to the comfort it provides; if it retains moisture, creates a smell, or otherwise adversely affects the atmosphere, it should be avoided.

■ With **'Dust-free' bedding** has to be judged objectively on the effect it has: a rim of black discharge at the nostrils is evidence that horses are inhaling dust.

■ With **Paper** is sometimes dusty, and will not provide good insulation on a cold floor; over rubber it is more effective. It needs to be deep, and regularly tended.

All varieties of bedding must be assessed objectively with the horse's health kept foremost: (*clockwise from top left*) rubberised matting; straw; paper; shavings

Stable Hygiene

The thrust of any stableyard routine must have the constant threat of disease in mind, and its procedures should minimise the chances of introducing or spreading infection. On this basis, a sensible attitude to hygiene is vital, particularly in a large yard or business concern.

A primary purpose of cleaning is the prevention of disease

IMPORTANT POINTS ON YARD HYGIENE

- Always keep in mind the fact that clothes, hands and utensils are one means of directly spreading infection.

- Be scrupulous about the cleanliness of feed bins, buckets and feed pots: wash and disinfect these on a regular basis; muck-sacks are inherently unhygienic and should not be allowed anywhere near feed.

- Beware of dirty handles on yard brushes, forks, shovels and wheelbarrows; clean routinely with a suitable disinfectant similar to Hibiscrub.

- Clean all grooming equipment between horses, especially in the presence of skin diseases such as ringworm, rain rash or external parasites.

- Treat horses coming back from competitions or race meetings as suspect carriers and isolate them; in particular limit any risk of spread by touch contact.

- Hygiene applies equally to transport vehicles and cars that may carry infection in from outside; be as clean as conditions allow, keep outside vehicles off the yard as far as possible; anticipate infection rather than have it enter through lack of thought.

By keeping records and being methodical a yard is run as a coherent enterprise, particularly the larger establishment. The following are reminders of what that entails:

In the morning

- Always start at a precise time, when horses will be given their first feed.
- Ventilate smelly stables immediately, and quickly skip out.
- Groom – though morning grooming is generally aimed at cleanliness only.
- Don't forget to pick the feet out.

After exercise

- Dry horses fully, and clean the legs; avoid excessive or unnecessary washing, as infection may establish itself while a horse is cold and wet.
- Never rug horses while they are wet; if absolutely necessary, use a sweat rug, or place a layer of straw between the horse and rug.
- Never let wet horses stand in their stables, unless under drying lights such as infra-reds.
- Skip out when you return, and provide fresh hay or feed (depending on dietary needs).
- Provide an hour at grass if at all possible, being mindful of the risks by limiting boisterousness and preventing fighting.

In the evening

- Set the horse up for the night with a fully clean bed.
- Groom thoroughly, strapping each limb thoroughly, and especially over the quarters and on the neck and shoulders.
- Consider the prevailing weather and adjust doors, windows and any vents accordingly.
- If the stable is cold, try to eliminate draughts; if too warm, provide adequate ventilation (but no more, except in warm climates where night-time temperatures stay high).
- Remember, many rugs will not help a horse standing in a draught; and horses in ideal stabling conditions will need fewer rugs and perhaps less food.
- Finally, fill in your records and sleep deeply.

Tack

- Be sure that all tack is clean, and never use tack from other horses without cleaning it.
- Remember that each horse is different in size, shape and weight, so make sure the tack you use fits the horse and does not lead to infection, back problems or sores.
- Don't use saddles that sit flat on the back and risk rubbing the withers, or girths that are too strong (new leather may inhibit free breathing if too tight).
- Always use your own tack at race meetings or in competitions.
- Clean any bridle if it is to be worn by another horse; disinfect the mouthpiece by dipping it into an appropriate solution.
- Protect the legs of jumpers, especially, with suitable boots, avoiding buckles and any type of fastener that can constrict blood flow.

Weather Influences

Energy in long-distance rides is often supplemented with wet sugar beet

TRAVEL

- Rug horses lightly for travel, and allow for the likelihood of sweating. Use electrolytes after arrival as indicated and required. The risk of bowel disturbance may indicate the use of probiotics to protect the natural organisms.

- Consider the risk of infection when sharing transport, and isolate horses after arrival for two to seven days, or longer, depending on where they have travelled from, and also the disease status at the point of origin.

- Horses are identified by their passports, and these must be kept in date, and be available for inspection at all times; they generally include drawings, verified by a vet, recording colour, markings, whorls, age, breed, sex and, sometimes, height; they may include photographs as well as recordings of vaccination and other data entered by the registering organisation. Microchips are now often an addition, as well as DNA tests on hair, and blood analysis to ensure the authenticity of any breeding recorded.

It goes without saying that varying climatic conditions require different working considerations. Horses competing in extremes of cold and warmth require special thought, as do those on long distance rides, be they in hot or temperate conditions.

Important Points

When working horses in extreme cold:

- Make sure to warm them up properly in order to avoid muscular injuries.
- Consider special shoeing for slippery surfaces, or to prevent balling, if riding on snow.
- Do not allow horses to drink water *ad lib* within an hour of competing.

On long distance rides (or drives)

- Horses are given a drink at their breakpoints, and sugar beet may be used as a carbohydrate source for horses likely to suffer extreme energy demands.
- Electrolytes are frequently used prior to competition, but should be provided in solution, or the horse allowed to drink afterwards, in order to prevent fluid transfer from other body systems into the gut.
- Veterinary checks at stop-points are critical, and dehydration is a special consideration; you can help by anticipating it.
- Horses over-heating in warm climates are hosed down to help cooling and to keep body temperatures stable; veterinary help will usually be available at a competition, and your horse will be monitored until he is fully recovered.
- Where there is a clinical problem with dehydration, fluids may be given intravenously.

Changing climate

Horses transferring from cold to warm climates may take time to acclimatise, and problems may be reflected in an inability to sweat. Those going in the opposite direction – from warm to cold climates (maybe changing seasonal patterns, as going from southern to northern hemispheres) – may suffer poor winter coat growth; the sensible response is to try and duplicate, or make up for, the changes, and to have patience with the horse as he adjusts.

13 DEALING WITH PROBLEMS

Advice on treating injuries, what to do in evident disease, or other routine ways of dealing with your horse's well-being are provided here on the strict understanding that clinical medicine is the field of qualified experts, and that every owner must know where to draw the line between what to do, and what not to do.

No emergency is ever experienced without anxiety and dread, but it is important to help the horse. Take colic as an example: horses in acute pain will often thrash about and throw themselves down with real violence, but it is often in their best interests to encourage them to stay on their feet, and the best way to do this is to keep them walking briskly. Often this is enough to let the trouble sort itself out, and some horses might even recover without further attention. When the vet arrives, the horse will be given drugs to quell pain and induce sedation. But your job will not be finished until you are sure that the crisis is completely over and the horse is fully recovered, with no danger of relapse.

Those dealing with horses on a daily basis will have a good idea of when the vet is needed, and when a condition can be safely dealt with. Superficial cuts and wounds can generally be treated without having to call your vet; so can filled legs, and most of the skin conditions mentioned on p150. Other situations require veterinary help as soon as possible: colic, systemic infections, nervous disorders. We will now discuss some of the more common conditions that might affect a horse's performance, indicating when veterinary assistance will probably be needed.

Acute pain, caused by colic	Keep the horse walking
Sick with temperature	Keep him warm and out of draughts
Wound that needs stitching	Stem the blood flow, and bandage if possible
Acute lameness with pain	Support the injured part, bandage any supporting leg
Foot penetration (nail)	Disinfect and bandage
Choke	Keep the horse on the move
Unable to stand	Keep him in a sitting position; offer a small drink
Acute diarrhoea	Keep him warm, offer water and electrolytes, and some good hay
Eye penetration	Bathe with warm water or Optrex

★ DIAGNOSING ILLNESS AND INFECTION ★

Refer to Chapter 5. Any systemic infection is likely to be accompanied by a temperature, and the horse will show general signs ranging from inappetance to depression and lassitude. Inevitably there will be a loss of form, a lack of energy, and reduced exercise tolerance. The more acute the condition, the more obvious are the signs, and the more important that you refer quickly to your vet.

Be sure to keep your horse warm and quiet, provide water and hay, and cut back on concentrates.

★ MONITORING THE HORSE'S WEIGHT ★

Checking on Weight Loss

- Make a routine examination of the membranes, glands and breathing.
- Consider worm status and have a faecal sample analysed.
- Make a detailed examination of the diet for quality as well as quantity.
- Ensure there is no dehydration.
- Scrutinise stable conditions, and especially temperature and airflows.
- If there are no obvious answers, call your vet.

Weight Gain

The most common reason for weight gain in an athletic horse would be improper or over-feeding, or inadequate exercise. It can also happen to a horse moved from cold to warm stabling and kept on the same diet, or to horses allowed to run at grass when there are sudden flushes of growth. Outside these parameters, weight gain is likely to be clinical and would have to be discussed with your vet.

★ WOUNDS THAT DO NOT REQUIRE STITCHING ★

- **FIRST**, stop any bleeding by application of pressure, by bandaging, or by using a ligature – though this must not stay on for longer than is necessary, and certainly not for more than an hour (and then with the advice of your vet anyway).
- Clean any dirt out using cotton wool, clean water and a mild disinfectant that won't irritate the tissues.
- Clip any hairs entering the wound, and if it is clean and dry, apply a wound powder and leave it open to the air. If you cannot get it completely clean, cover it with a sterile dressing, or poultice it, especially if it is weeping and contaminated by grit or dirt.
- **IF THERE IS INFECTION**, poultice the wound, and speak to your vet; if it isn't clearing, antibiotics may be needed. Always make sure of tetanus cover.
- Allow as much air to get at a wound as is possible. To this end, remove dressings at least every day, and preferably twice daily; if there is no infection, try to get all dressings off fully after three to four days: air is critical to healing, and if it is occluded, anaerobic organisms proliferate. Exceptions are when there is infection, and when support is needed to hold a wound together: in which case your vet will advise.
- **ULTRASOUND TREATMENT** may be appropriate and beneficial in some cases. Where there is no infection it should be applied after the wound is 24 hours old. Use for about one minute, 1–2cm (½in) back from the wound's edge on pulse mode. Repeat daily moving closer

Minor injuries can be hosed with clean, cold water to reduce the swelling

Apply a pressure bandage to stop bleeding where necessary, but never for more than an hour

to the edges each time. If there is an infection, wait until normal healing is well under way. If proud flesh is noticed it can be treated directly (taking advice on strengths and frequencies) on a daily basis.

(*left*) Proud flesh can be effectively treated with ultrasound or laser

IN THE EVENT OF INJURY

There are certain things that should be observed as a matter of course:

*If the injury affects a leg, do not use supporting bandages on other limbs except when absolutely necessary; and if you do have to, then remove them every twelve hours and massage the legs.

*Be aware that any bandage can cause problems by interfering with the blood flow, which can cause sloughing; be careful to apply it evenly, and never over-tighten.

*Reduce the concentrate feed.

*Return to exercise judiciously, making the horse walk gently in hand even the day after injury where possible; the repair needs to be made strong and able to withstand movement, so only confine a horse where your vet insists it is necessary.

*Return to full feeding gradually, using the occasional linseed mash to keep the gut moving.

★ NERVOUS SIGNS ★

Any indication of wobbling where there is a possibility of infection or poisoning requires immediate veterinary attention, as do acute nervous signs after a fall. Gradually progressive nervous symptoms, when the horse is healthy, eating and in no distress, will still need investigation; refer to the general advice already given in Chapters 9 and 10, as well as those relating to feeding, dehydration and nursing.

Horses that have been recumbent due to EHV 1 paralysis may be supported in slings and will need continued daily nursing until they can stand again on their own. If not supported, they will develop skin ulcers, and may lose the will and the strength to get back up on their feet.

★ WHEN THERE IS FEVER ★

This is nearly always a situation where you should call your vet; make sure the horse is kept warm and out of draughts before he/she comes. For the duration of the illness:

- provide water and hay;
- use electrolytes routinely, even when there is no evident sweating;
- reduce concentrate feeding, and give only small, sloppy mashes.
- As soon as there is recovery, return gently to work: take for a long walk first, and if there are no adverse reactions, trot the next day; increase the workload gradually as long as the horse is coping. Canter gently for several days before galloping, if the horse's training routine demands fast work.

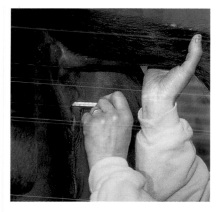

(left) Take the temperature as a routine when you first suspect infection

★ FILLED LEGS ★

General filling around the fetlocks of maybe just the hind legs, or all four, often denotes a circulatory problem. Sometimes it reflects digestive upset, when there will be no heat and no pain; in this case check the diet and reduce concentrate intake, and provide a bran or linseed mash. The condition is often benign and may pass off quickly, but if it doesn't disappear with exercise, consult your vet.

Filling in individual legs may be associated with wounds and abrasions, in which case it usually occurs above the injured area. As long as there is no infection, these respond well to either laser or ultrasound treatment; if there is any doubt about infection, however, do not treat it yourself, but speak to your vet.

Lymphangitis is an extreme filling of usually a single limb; of obscure causation, it requires veterinary attention; in this case, the leg may be painful to touch.

149

Rain rash (right):

will clear up through scab removal and application of a non-irritant disinfectant such as hibitane. Bring the horse in from the wet and keep the skin dry; if the condition appears to be resistant, speak to your vet.

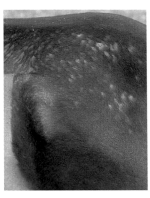

Ringworm (left):

is a very contagious condition usually marked by circular lesions; speak to your vet who will provide washes or griseofulvin, a powder that is given by mouth for a minimum of seven days. Most forms also infect humans, so it is advisable to take certain precautions:

- handle infected animals with care;
- wash hands in disinfectant after every contact;
- avoid spread on clothing, tack, feeding utensils, grooming kit and so on;
- isolate affected horses, and tend to them last;
- disinfect stables between horses.

Sweet Itch (right):

can be identified by the horse rubbing and scratching the tail and mane, sometimes until these parts are raw and bleeding. It occurs in affected horses during the fly season, especially in marshy, downland areas, being an allergic response to the bite of the Culicoides midge. One or more of the following procedures may be tried to alleviate the condition:

- surface treatments may ease the irritation, though results are disappointing in severe cases;
- protective clothing works for some;
- keep affected horses in screened stables at dawn and dusk;
- fly repellents may help.

Mud Fever (right):

typically occurs in the pastern area, and more commonly on skin that is not pigmented, though it may occur on any leg, and it often extends higher. The condition may be resolved by observing the following procedures:

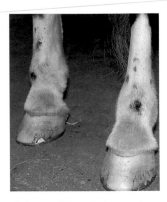

- try to keep the horse out of the conditions that caused the problem, including unsanitary bedding;
- clean off scabs (applying baby oil to them 6–8 hours earlier to soften the scabs will make them much easier to remove) and apply a healing lotion, or an antibiotic-based ointment such as Dermobion (from your vet);
- more severe cases, with badly swollen legs, may need a course of antibiotic injections;
- gentle exercise will help to reduce swelling;
- the repairing legs may need to be protected by bandages until healed.

Lice:

can generally be seen as tiny, moving white specks, usually in a long, dirty coat. They may be the cause of severe scratching and weight loss, and can be indicative of lack of condition, poor health and bad management. Treat with antiparasitic washes or louse powder, repeated in two weeks; also treat 'in-contacts', and contaminated surfaces in protracted cases.

Warts:

are common on the muzzle, are not serious and will usually self-cure.

Melanomas:

are pigment tumours of the skin, and should be seen by your vet; they can spread and are potentially serious.

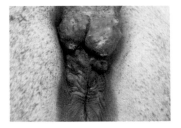

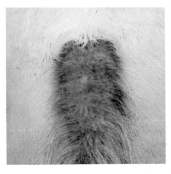

(*above*) Melanoma in the anal region and (*left*) sarcoid

Sarcoids

are troublesome, especially when they get rubbed by tack; you should see your vet about possible removal.

★ COLIC ★

The predominant sign in colic is pain. As the condition develops, there may be dullness, a reluctance to eat, perhaps brief bouts of pawing, or the horse may lie down and roll. These signs may become progressively worse, and would be accompanied by increasing violence along with a growing tendency to self-destruction. The milder the condition the lower the level of pain; the more critical the cause – such as acute bowel distension, a twisted gut, or maybe even an aneurysm – the more violent the horse becomes, and the more frightening for everyone involved trying to save him.

What to Do

- From the outset, try to keep the horse on his feet and moving; it is always best to prevent any violent reaction that might exacerbate the condition or cause irreparable injury; even a gentle roll in a sand ring might compound a twist and is best prevented if possible.
- The vet will provide immediate pain-killing injections, sedation, and probably antispasmodics.
- Surgery is the best hope for twists, aneurysms and any kind of complete obstruction; the success rate has improved, and bowel resections are possible using modern operating procedures.
- The percentage success is high in cases where there isn't either a twist, an aneurysm or a complete blockage, which means relief in spasmodic colic, impaction and constipation.
- Recurrent colic is sometimes a sign of chronic worm infestation, and may pass off in time with regular dosing and if the horse is taken off infected land. However, it could also be a sign of early grass sickness, which will need diagnosis and treatment by your vet; this condition is nearly always fatal.

Aftercare

- After treatment, there is an ongoing burden of care: the colicy horse has to be stayed with and supervised closely until fully recovered, which means making sure its problems are not just being masked by drugs.
- Appetite is a good indicator of recovery, and the sequence of events (especially in spasmodic colic) is often a release of gas, perhaps for anything up to an hour, accompanied by a gradual return of appetite and the passing off of drug effects. Nevertheless, although release of gas is

often a welcome sign, it is not necessarily an indication of recovery, and the horse should always be watched in case of relapse. It is generally safe for him to pick at hay, although this would not be sensible in cases such as stoppage, when extra food volume might only increase pain; your vet will advise on this.

- Recovering from surgery is a more protracted matter, and requires the provision of non-irritant food that will not cause the breakdown of internal repair; advice on this will be provided by your vet. Full recovery, even when parts of the bowel have been removed, is increasingly common, although there may be an ongoing dietary limitation afterwards to avoid recurring problems.

★ CHOKE ★

Choke is marked by profuse salivation, coughing and pain, and is indicated by the horse stretching out his neck in a deserate effort to bring the obstructing material back up the gullet. In the past, a typical cause was the eating of large chunks of potato or turnip, or similar.

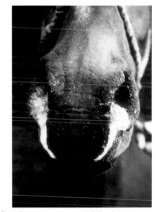

Choke can also occur on dry food eaten too quickly that sticks in the gullet because it hasn't been chewed sufficiently, and so not enough saliva has been produced to lubricate its passage.

What to Do

- If a swelling is seen along the left side of the neck, massage it gently to try and disperse or move it; do not use force.
- A drink might move it, although the horse is unlikely to drink.
- The vet may pass a stomach tube, or simply sedate the horse and wait.
- It is unusual for horses to die from choke, although the condition is dramatic and needs immediate attention; the greatest risk is often the horse's tendency to panic, which may induce shock. With patience, many cases recover with no ill effects.

★ DIARRHOEA ★

Diarrhoea in foals is a common problem that is normally successfully treated (except where there are immunity problems). Adult diarrhoea is less common, however, and perhaps a greater worry because of the volumes of fluid lost and the implications for the horse if this loss is not quickly stemmed. Acute diarrhoea, as in colitis X, can be quickly fatal, or the horse may even be found dead. There is a suspicion that the condition is caused by sudden dietary change, and it is not uncommon where horses are changed from poor to rich grazing too abruptly. In the spring or autumn the possibility that worms are the cause should also be considered.

What to Do

- Stop all solid feeding and provide only hay and water.
- Provide electrolytes using an effective preparation (if the horse won't drink, your vet will dose by stomach tube, or inject through the vein).
- Water quantities consumed must equal those lost, and electrolyte quantities must relate to fluid consumption.
- Where there is evident depression, get your vet, or if the condition lasts more than a few hours.
- In the spring or autumn, treat for worms.

★ EYE INFECTIONS ★

Many eye infections are noticed when the eye clouds over; the most common cause is a thorn prick, or some sort of direct trauma.

What to Do

- Bathe with warm water and a non-irritating solution such as Optrex. As long as the effect on the horse is mild and there is an easing of discomfort, recovery should be uncomplicated. If it is otherwise, speak to your vet.

★ COUGHING ★

Coughing occurs as a result of specific infectious diseases such as flu. It can occur from lungworm, especially where horses graze the same ground as donkeys. It can also occur as a result of draughty stabling conditions where the horse can find no escape from often insidious airflows that seem insignificant to stable staff. The important matter is to get veterinary advice and seek the cause so it can be reversed – though be aware that many coughs clear up without the use of drugs; also that there is a great deal that management may do by way of creating greater comfort and eliminating conditions that irritate the respiratory passages.

More serious is the condition known as 'COPD', also called 'broken wind'. This is an allergic problem that leads to progressive lung damage and increased breathing rates, and is typified by a deep cough that is seldom fully cured. Symptoms can be reduced, however, and with proper management horses may then become useful riding animals again.

What to Do Against COPD

- Always ensure there is adequate air in the stable without draughts (remembering that infection on top of an allergy can only make matters worse).
- Keep the atmosphere dust free, and remove cobwebs.
- Clean all contact areas and feed pots.
- Use dust-free, non allergenic bedding, avoiding straw (paper on a rubber base maybe).
- Feed good clean silage in preference to hay.
- Long, steady canter work is preferable to sprints in order to increase endurance fitness without taxing the lungs – but only if your vet says the horse can take it.
- Train from the field if unsuccessful from the stable, providing shelter and New Zealand rugs.
- Your vet will provide drugs, such as Ventipulmin, that may help relieve the symptoms and make riding more possible in extreme cases – but *be aware* that these drugs may not be usable in competition.
- Remember that COPD is an allergic condition, and that inevitably best results come from keeping the horse away from the cause.

14 SPECIAL DISEASE CONSIDERATIONS

Each equestrian sport has its own protocols, training regimes and disease controls. These may vary simply from flu vaccination to the more complex regulations that now apply to racing, which may well include veterinary inspection of animals in order to preclude contagious infection and to ensure lame horses are not allowed to race. A further aspect of this care is the checks made during the course of riding and driving events and endurance rides. Horses are not llowed to continue that are lame, have high heart rates or are dehydrated. In this chapter we will outline aspects of disease control that should always be kept in mind when infection is rife.

General Observations

The implications for any other infectious condition can be drawn from these examples, remembering that any return to work after illness needs to be progressive and conducted with great patience; it should also be properly monitored, and in the full knowledge of any influence likely to cause permanent damage to critical organs such as the heart, liver and lungs, if only as a measure of safety for future riding. Also consider the possibility of new infections in debilitated horses, and the risk of spreading disease to others that are susceptible.

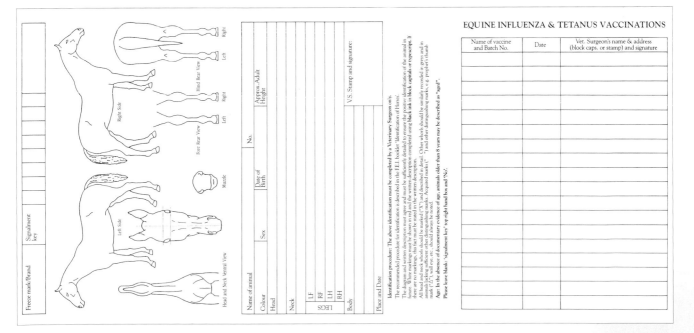

Record of equine vaccination

Equine Influenza and Tetanus

Flu vaccination is compulsory for many equestrian disciplines, and the regulations fall along a common path in virtually all cases. Records are kept on passports (or similar documents) that include identification and veterinary verification of vaccination details. These are critical documents that have to be produced on demand for inspection at any event or race meeting; they must be kept with care, and must always be up to date, otherwise your horse will be sent home without being allowed to compete.

SIGNS OF FLU

- High temperature, inappetance and coughing.
- Rapid spread in a group of horses; incubation periods approx 1–3 days.
- Depression.
- Great discomfort; may be reluctant to move, simply standing with head stuck out and coughing painfully.
- Copious white nasal discharges that may last for weeks.
- Spread by coughing, mostly direct from horse to horse; also thought to be carried on the wind over considerable distances.
- The nature of the discharges, being thick and pussy, lends itself to spread by hand, utensils, clothing and vehicles.
- Recovery is slow.
- Pneumonia may occur as a secondary complication.

WHAT TO DO

- **Abandon work routines until recovery complete** as the influence on trained horses is absolute.
- **Be aware** that even for vaccinated horses, extreme caution is needed as there is always the possibility of a milder illness, without pronounced coughing and visible discharges. Vaccine failure is also known, so there can be no certainty, as with any disease, and the risk of spread must be considered.
- **Consult your vet immediately.** Diagnosis can be extremely quick with modern methods of testing. Follow veterinary advice regarding exercise restraint, feeding, contact with other horses, and return to normal work.
- **Isolate affected horses.** After contact, disinfect all equipment and your own footwear; wear a separate set of clothes.
- **Rest recovered horses for at least three weeks** and allow to regain any lost weight before being returned to work.

VACCINATION RULES FOR FLU

- Two initial injections given at an interval of 21–90 days.
- Third injection is given between 150 and 215 days after the second.
- Subsequently an annual injection will be needed.
- Injections must be in order on the horse's passport, along with the type of vaccine, the batch number, the place and date given, vet's signature, and a formal identification of the horse.

TETANUS

- Tetanus prevention is a wise precaution and can be given together with the flu jab and recorded on the passport.
- Vaccination begins with two injections three weeks apart followed by an annual (or biannual) booster, depending on the vaccine type, and also the recommendations of your vet.

Typical signs of tetanus: note the stiff, splayed stance and the visible third eyelid

EHV-1 The significance of this disease to athletic horses has changed significantly in modern times due to the nature of the virus and the manner in which it has its effects. It is primarily a respiratoy infection that has an insidious and debilitating course.

SIGNS OF EHV-1

- Incubation period is 2–10 days.
- Watery nasal discharge evident at the nostrils at an early stage.
- The horse may cough or, more commonly, snort the discharge out.
- There is a tinge of yellow most easily seen in the eye membranes when the liver is infected
- Staggering may occur and is extremely serious as it may lead to recumbency, although these symptoms are more common in broodmares than in athletic horses; however, working affected horses might precipitate nervous signs.
- Temperature may rise in the early stages of infection, though it may not, either: it tends to be very variable, often going up and down even on the same day. In fact the signs of EHV 1 are all generally rather nebulous, and may be hard to follow in the early stages.
- Diagnosis is made by blood serum analysis and virus isolation.
- Virus is spread through the discharges, and the nasal discharge is expressed like an aerosol onto the wind when the horse coughs or snorts.

WHAT TO DO

- Keep the horse warm.
- Eliminate fast work.
- Reduce feeding, especially protein levels.
- Have patience and do not return to work too quickly.
- Restore lost condition before full work resumed.
- If a horse has been recumbent give him a break at grass before resuming ridden work.
- Support recumbent horses in slings.
- Feed sloppy foods when appetite is poor and provide cut grass.
- Maintain gut health with washes and/or probiotics
- Give electrolytes orally
- Seek plenty of advice from your vet

PROGNOSIS

- Leaves affected horses susceptible to other infections as they recover.
- Virus persists in the bodies of recovered animals and can set up repeat infections, although the precise practical effects of this are unclear; they may be largely influenced by standards of management.
- Efficacy of vaccine in preventing clinical disease is frequently disappointing.
- Abortion is a common feature in broodmares, and foals may be born infected and die. The problems for trained horses suffering EHV 1 are compounded because the liver and nervous system are affected.

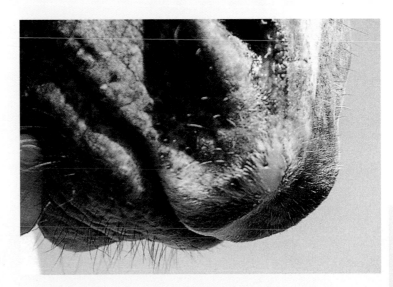

In the equine herpes virus a watery nasal discharge, which becomes thicker and grey-yellow in colour, is visible

EVA This is a highly infectious viral disease, with coughing a predominant sign of its respiratory influences. The condition is common in North America and Europe, and poses a particular difficulty in control because of the manner in which it is spread. Transmission is by direct contact, by droplet infection, and by stallions in their semen. Drinking water may become contaminated and be a means of spread, as may bedding, feed pots and so on. Good hygiene is therefore critical in control. Infected stallions may remain virus shedders for years through their semen, and pose a special problem in efforts to prevent spread; one of the risks is that covered fillies going into racing and competition yards may set up new infections. In the USA, however, this is considered to be a disease of Saddlebreds and Standardbreds, not of Thoroughbreds, where only a 2 per cent infection rate has been recognised. Diagnosis is by serum analysis and virus isolation.

SIGNS OF EVA

- Incubation period is 2–15 days.
- Flu-like symptoms with temperature, depression and coughing.
- Filling of the limbs is common because of the effect on circulation.
- The disease was once known as 'pink eye' because of inflammation of the eye membranes and swelling of the eyelids.
- The skin is affected by rashes and plaques.
- Soft swellings (oedema) are also seen on the udder and scrotum.
- Mares may abort at any stage of pregnancy.
- Spreads more slowly than flu, though the influences in affected animals can be worse; these vary, too, some horses showing only the mildest symptoms, while the disease may be fatal to others

WHAT TO DO

- **Isolate your horse when you get home** should you have been to any event or meeting where infection was present. There is no cross-immunity between diseases such as flu and EVA or EHV.
- **Do not continue with normal training programme.** For horses in any sort of intensive training, and particularly involving fast work, cut back to steady canters; it is important that your horse doesn't sweat from exertion.
- **Reduce concentrate feeding.**
- **Observe horse closely for seven to ten days.**
- **Call your vet quickly** if there are any signs of infection, such as watery eyes or nose, membrane colour changes, coughing, or filling of the legs. In particular look out for any untoward changes in temperament, appetite and exercise tolerance.

PROGNOSIS

- Problems from EVA in trained horses will depend on the extent to which the infection debilitates an individual animal; however, the consequences even for those displaying only the mildest of symptoms are likely to be serious when they return to full training, and would need careful monitoring; heart problems could be anticipated. Moreover the potential for changes to any virus means there should be no complacency – and the way clinical virus disease is constantly changing today means there is always a potential for new expressions of disease.
- For any athletic horse, a severe attack would, in all probability, mean the loss of months rather than weeks of training; and it is a potentially lethal infection. Each case should be taken on its merits and monitored closely, but physical recovery will be slow. Confer regularly with your vet.
- There is no point in vaccinating an infected horse, nor are there any usable drugs effective against viruses at present.
- Once recovered, affected horses are immune from future attacks of EVA.

Vaccination

There are vaccines available: in the USA a modified virus vaccine has proved effective, and a dead vaccine in use in the UK and Ireland is also working. Vaccination will depend on the threat of infection, and the controls in operation in any country; for those hoping to compete abroad, it would be as well to check on import and export regulations: speak to your vet. Note, too, that before using the dead vaccine, blood tests may be needed to ensure that a horse has not previously been infected; for horses that are required to have a passport, this then has to be recorded in it, along with vaccination details.

STRANGLES For any owner, the experience of watching a horse going through the clinical stages of strangles is distressing. It is a slow and insidious condition caused by a bacterium, and characterised by gross swelling of the lymph glands in the head region, their rupture, and the release of thick pus that sometimes seems to go on forever. The pus is the means of transmission, and the condition is very contagious to horses that come in contact with it.

Diagnosis depends on isolation of the bacterium from infected pus.

SIGNS OF STRANGLES

- Incubation period is 7–10 days, though this is shortened in bad outbreaks where a number of horses are involved, and may vary from as low as two days, to three weeks.
- Initial high temperature and watery discharge that soon becomes purulent.
- Signs of a sore throat may be evident at the start, marked by difficulty in swallowing.
- Glands in the throat area swell and become hot and painful before rupturing.
- Recovery may be quick after this, or the glands may continue to discharge for days or weeks; symptoms may last for from one week to over two months.
- The organism is transmitted through the discharges, and these can contaminate stables, utensils, feed pots and so on; they can get onto yard brush handles, taps and buckets, and also hands and clothes.
- There is also a carrier state, and some symptomless horses can carry the organism and set up infection when moving into fresh populations.
- Infection can be picked up in fields, and not just from fresh infection; the organism may persist for up to nine weeks after contamination; and individual animals will shed the organism for as long as eight months after recovery.

WHAT TO DO

- **Once infection has got on to a pasture stop using for at least two to three months .**
- **Confine infected horses to stables where they were tended last.**
- **Infected horses should have their own feed buckets as well as any other utensils or equipment.**
- **Be critical about hygiene, personal as well as general.** Disinfect hands and boots every time an infected horse is attended.
- **Keep disinfectant footbaths convenient** for easy dipping of boots outside stables.
- **Return to exercise gradually,** or provide a recovery period at grass before any attempt is made to restart a training programme.

PROGNOSIS

- **This disease has serious implications for the athletic horse**. It leads to loss of condition, and it can be fatal in severe cases, the horse dying from pneumonia and other internal complications. All external signs of infection need to have disappeared before a horse is ridden again.
- **An apparently recovered horse may still shed infection** that could get onto tack, or still be directly transmitted by hand to others previously unaffected.

Swelling of the throat, typically seen in cases of strangles

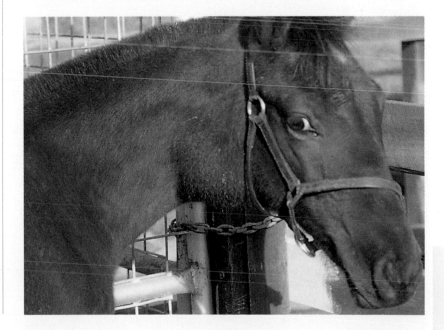

INDEX

ILLUSTRATIVE ACKNOWLEDGEMENTS

All photographs by Kit Houghton except:
Andrew Carter: 76(all), 89
David & Charles/Kit Houghton: pp21, 40top left&rt, 53(colour images only), 54(all), 83
David & Charles/Bob Langrish: pp11, 31btm left&rt, 32top&btm, 33(all), 101, 107, 109, 112
Peter Gray: pp22btm, 43btm (by permission of EPC, Unit 1, Deverill Trading Estate, Warminster, BA12 7BZ, UK and Mustad Hoofcare SA, 2 Rue de l'Industrie, Bulle 1630, Switzerland), 76(all), 89, 92–3,

140(sweet itch, melanoma and sarcoid images), 153
Dr Derek Knottenbelt/University of Liverpool Department of Veterinary Clinical Science and Animal Husbandry: pp46(all), 50
Gill O'Donnell: page 53(b/w image)
Tony & Marcy Pavord: pp154, 155
Colin Vogel: pp150(ringworm), 151, 157

All artworks by Maggie Raynor except:
Paul Bale/Visual Image: pp73, 82, 106, 123
Sam Elmhurst: pp113, 115btm left&rt, 117
Eva Melhuish: pp27, 100–1btm row, 126